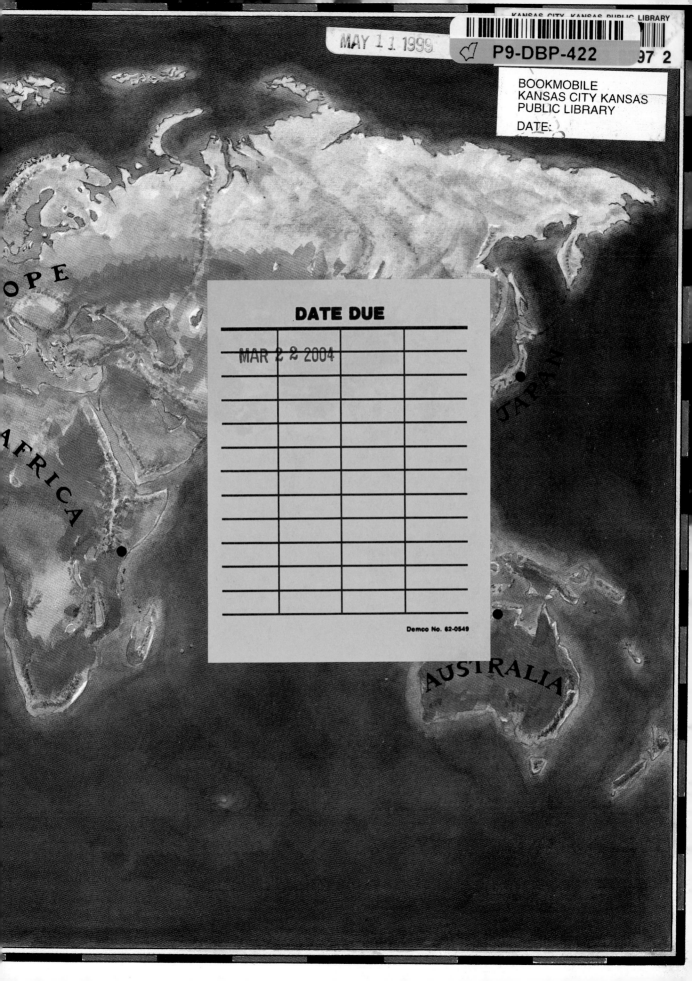

Birds
of the
Wetlands

A pair of African Fish Eagles.

Birds
of the
Wetlands

James Hancock

Academic Press
London

AP Natural World is published by
ACADEMIC PRESS
525 B Street, Suite 1900, San Diego,
California 92101-4495, USA
http://www.apnet.com

ACADEMIC PRESS
24-28 Oval Road
London NW1 7DX
http://www.hbuk.co.uk/ap/

A catalogue record for this book is available from the British Library

ISBN 0-12-322727-5

Printed in Spain

99 00 01 02 03 MC 9 8 7 6 5 4 3 2 1

Cover illustrations:
Front: Snowy Egret
Back: Bald Eagle

Contents

Roseate Spoonbill, Florida Everglades.

Foreword

The world of wetlands is a nearly unfathomable one. They are so complex ecologically that no one fully understands what makes them work. By turns they are wet or dry; they are deep or shallow; they are full of plants or unvegetated; they are rich with oxygen or they are deoxygenated to the extreme; they are full of wildlife or they are depauperate – perhaps experiencing all of these within a few short months. Is it any wonder that they are so easily misunderstood by their local neighbours, or by scientists and conservationists?

Hundreds of millions of people interact with wetlands daily. Most live in them, or by them, or venture briefly into them to take their fish and game or raw materials. Thousands are active in their conservation worldwide. Others are studying them at all scales. For all their importance to civilization, for all the many studies done and for all those conservation plans developed, we understand them poorly. Quantifying their complexity, their variability and their changeability exceeds our capacity to know them analytically. As years pass we will understand more, but as years pass we will lose more and more as the wetland resources we know so poorly are drained, flooded and otherwise fundamentally changed by man's hand.

There are times when understanding requires more than analyses. It takes experience; it takes being there; it takes a sense of place and perspective that only time allows; it takes capturing the essences in an image or a few salient words. I am convinced that one can in some sense know more about a lily pond from Monet than from a text book.

This is a book of that sort. It is a book of experience, of reflection and of intuition. It is a book that captures essences of great wetlands in stories of the birds and of the lives of the people, in the traditions of human societies, in the understanding of past trends and future prospects and in photographic images of the place, especially in images of the essential creatures of wetland, the birds.

James Hancock comes to his task from a lifetime of 'being there'. He created for himself the opportunities to visit the great wetlands of the world, many repeatedly, over the course of years and decades. He got to know the people and the places, and especially the birds. His photographs are not just pretty pictures, they are the vignettes that hint at the underlying truths of what a wetland is.

Mr Hancock has held many offices and received many awards for his ornithological works, not least the Order of the British Empire from Her Majesty the Queen and medals and prizes from scientific societies. But his greatest reward is that of sharing his insights, his experiences and his vision with others, especially with the younger generation of conservationists, those not yet jaded by the losses he has seen in his decades of observing.

Some of these stories were first written a decade ago. Some of what Mr Hancock foresaw has come about in the interim. Some of the stories are new. All are the product of his great labours over a lifetime of conservation work and of his great love for the natural world. Read the stories, look at the images and begin to appreciate the unfathomable complexity, the subtle beauty and the impending losses of wetlands and their birds.

James A Kushlan
Director
Patuxent Institute, U.S.A.
October 1997

Introduction

Wetland areas are subject to many changes. They are drained to provide farming or building land. They are polluted by chemicals or sewage. They are harvested or burnt. They are sailed in, fished on, or shot over. Finally, some are apparently saved only for it to be discovered that their source of water has been either diverted or polluted. This means not complete destruction, but a long lingering period of despair. It becomes evident that the wetland area itself and its surrounding environment form an integral part of what is invariably a complex and fragile ecosystem. Without a complete infrastructure this is inevitably fractured.

Much of the destruction and all the major attempts at conservation have occurred in the last 25 years. Only in very recent years has it become apparent that species protection is totally useless without suitable habitat.

During most of these explosive years, I have been a witness to the changes that have taken place in many diverse wetland areas. My fascination with herons and their allies has drawn me to every continent of the globe, and I have returned to many of the world's great wetland regions again and again.

By describing an area of wetland and its birds in each major region, I have tried to show the development of these once unknown swamps to their present status as part of a dwindling number of increasingly rare and ecologically important wetland habitats. These feed and house a multitude of the world's birds, many of which are close to extinction. Each of these regions, which it has been my good fortune to visit, presents a different scene and yet they all have much in common. Even the birds of the wetlands reflect their differences and similarities.

In the decade since I wrote about the regions described in this book, all of them have, by their very nature, been subjected to seemingly never-ending threats of one sort or another upon their inevitably fragile ecosystems. To sustain such wetland areas requires continual vigilance and it is clear that most of them, without sophisticated modern management, are unlikely to survive. Even in Florida's Everglades the learning curve is as steep as ever. Each country has its own problems, but none more so than those countries of the Far East beyond India.

Sadly, few of these cultures have attempted either locally or nationally to preserve their wildlife or its habitat in the face of the advancing tide of the human race, or to consider the environmental cost of their rapidly expanding economic growth.

The sheer devastation of wetlands, of forests, of rivers and of coastlines continues unabated and indeed accelerates at a frightening rate. Such destruction is usually the result of indifference, of ignorance, or of greed. Here too, the demand increases for medical stimulants which cruelly purport to transfer to humans the beauty or strength perceived in wild creatures. That a peasant woman steals the egg of a beautifully plumed egret in the belief that it will enhance her appeal, is one thing, but the wholesale slaughter of creatures to provide imagined aphrodisiacs is quite another.

Although in India all these pressures do exist, and there is little official concern expressed today as to the consequences to the wildlife of their rapidly expanding population, there is, in this unique Asian land, a deep-seated ethical and cultural concern for all creatures, amongst many of its communities, sects and creeds which transcends the indifference of the political establishment. For this reason I have included in this second volume two such instances of this behaviour, one in the east and one in the west of this subcontinent to highlight the effect that this benign interaction can have on the welfare of the birds around them.

Nethertheless the recent disaster, which may well damage the Coto Doñana for decades to come, highlights the apparent inability of governments to afford protection even to an area designated as a World Heritage Site.

Finally away from tropical lands, I have pictured that remarkable lake in Iceland where birds from both Europe and America breed side by side in quite astonishing numbers. It is here that the first astronauts practiced their skilld before rocketing to the moon!

Improbable though it may seem, in the ever-shrinking wetlands some birds are, against the odds, doing very well as a result of such behaviour.

Tricolor Heron.

Acknowledgements

In the first volume of this book I acknowledged any indebtedness to many friends all over the world. I must offer my thanks in this edition to those who were of such help in the writing of three new chapters.

Tragically, in Gujarat, one of India's most talented teachers, Professor R M Naik, who had been responsible for the training of some of India's brightest ornithologists, died before our work on Reef Herons could be completed. Additionally his mentor, and my friend, Shivraj Kumar Khachar of Jasdan, also died at far too early an age. Such talented people are rare in Asia, and they will be greatly missed.

Happily, in Assam, Professor P C Bhattercharjee spreads his engaging enthusiasm throughout that troubled state and his assistant Prasant Saikia has played a leading part in one of the exciting discoveries made in India in recent years.

Icleandic airlines were my hosts on my journey to this spectacular island, where the last Great Auks were killed, but now 'when the first whimbrel arrives the sun will start shining and the flowers bloom' as Páll Olafsson's poem describes the spring.

I have also received a great deal of help from many of the distinguished members of the Colonial Water Birds Society. This society has, in 20 years, become the world's leading organization in conservation and scientific study of birds of the wetlands.

Finally I continue to receive support from Dr James Kushlan. His help and encouragement has been invaluable.

Of course without that globe-trotting editor of Academic Press Dr Andrew Richford this book would not have seen the light of day and my thanks!

The Green-backed Heron is adept at
catching small fish from unlikely
perches like this mooring rope.

1 North America

The Florida Everglades

In 1949, two years after the Everglades were dedicated a National Park, Charles M Brookfield wrote, with Oliver Griswold, a book entitled *They All Called it Tropical*. This modest little paperback has a foreword by Daniel Beard, the Park's first Superintendent, and an introduction by John Pennekamp, one of Florida's pioneer conservationists, who was at that time Associate Editor of the *Miami Herald* and Chairman of the Park Commission.

All these famous names are those of the men associated with the beginnings of the greatest of all wetland National Wildlife Parks in America.

Charlie Brookfield was the last of the great National Audubon wardens in Florida, and in the copy which he gave me of his book he wrote: 'To my good friend Jim Hancock on the occasion of his first visit to Cape Sable, 1963'.

It has been my good fortune to spend some time in this magnificent wetlands park nearly every year since. I have thus been able to observe its development, to exult over its triumphs and to agonize over its disasters, during these changing years of fortune.

Charlie put this wilderness and its turbulent history into perspective for me. His book gives the history of the Everglades since the early Indian days, but his knowledge of the birds and their unique habitats, told to me as we wandered by boat through the keys, many of which he named, has left a lasting impression.

Since that time, many of the scientists and Park officials have, over the years, helped to widen and deepen my knowledge of this extraordinary and complex wetland, and the process has continued until today.

Key West is the most southerly of the protecting line of keys – or islands – which form a curtain eastwards around Florida Bay. It lies 1° north of the Tropic of Cancer, so that the keys, and the Everglades on the mainland to the north of them, are virtually tropical in climate and vegetation. In this swampland, rainfall is seasonal; about 85% of it falls between May and October, so that, from November to the end of April, the water levels progressively drop and the marshes and swamps dry out.

This swampland covers nearly 7 million acres (2.8 million ha), of which 1.4 million (0.56 million) are a National Park. Barely above sea level, the saucer-shaped Lake Okeechobee spilled over on to the sawgrass plains and

Bald Cypress (*Taxedium distichum*) is the home of a large variety of wetland birds, as well as alligators, turtles and a wealth of fish species.

This Great White Egret has caught a Florida scrub lizard. The diet of this large Egret consists mainly of fish, crustaceans and small reptiles, but it will eat insects, young birds, and a wide variety of small mammals.

The Wood Stork is America's only stork, and like most storks throughout the world has found it harder than herons to adjust to changes in wetland habitat brought about by man. This bird is in full courtship plumage.

drained slowly southwards to the sea. The land fall is about 3 inches in every mile (41mm per km), and the flat open grassland is dotted with mangroves and 'hammocks' of hardwood, with occasional stands of Caribbean pine *Pinus caribaea* on higher ground. This natural flow persisted until early drainage canals were developed into intricate drainage schemes which have changed the ecology of the area for ever.

Southern Florida was a wild, inhospitable land, inhabited by alligators, crocodiles, snakes and insects. The coast, hot and humid during the rainy season, was struck every few years by hurricanes, which tore up trees, destroying huge tracts of vegetation and flooding the land.

In the 15th century the Spanish explorer, Ponce de Leon, discovered this wilderness during his vain search for the 'Fountain of Youth'. He found the Calusa Indians living in small, highly mobile bands, each group joined by canals built to take their canoes swiftly through the swamps. Fleets of these canoes, capable of travelling as far as Cuba, attacked the first Spanish ships, including that of de Leon. By 1597, Spanish missionaries had sufficient influence over this aggressive tribe to make certain that their plundering of ships and shipwrecks was confined to those of the British and Americans.

Many years later, the British joined the Creek Indians from Georgia and north Florida (a tribe later to be called Seminoles) and forced out the majority of Calusa. By 1763 Spain ceded Florida to Britain, but of such little value did it appear to be at that time that it was later returned to Spain in exchange for the Bahamas. Throughout the period, both Indians and early European settlers plundered and pirated passing ships. It was after the United States acquired the territory that the combined forces of America, Spain and

The Snowy Egret is a lively small all-white egret. When breeding it has plumes on its neck and back and sports long thick feathers on its head. Its yellow skin behind the black bill turns red at the time and so do its yellow feet. It is often called the bird with the yellow toes.

Britain were brought to bear on defeating the thousands of men, and over 100 ships, pirating these seaways.

The wonders of the wildlife of the little-known wilderness were undiscovered until revealed by the famous American artist John James Audubon. His paintings done in this region are today the most highly prized of all bird paintings, fetching astronomical figures when they appear on the market. Soon after his death, however, the infamous plume trade began. The apparently insatiable demands of high fashion in Paris, London and New York for 'aigrettes' demanded the slaughter of hundreds of thousands of the nesting herons, egrets and seabirds, not only here in Florida, but all over the world.

Soon after the trade reached its peak the first railroad was driven through the Everglades; by the beginning of the 20th century land was being drained for farming, fishing was commercially exploited and the march of civilization had begun. By then, however, the need to conserve as well as to exploit had become apparent, and the efforts of conservationists, led by a land purchase by the Florida Federation of Women's Clubs, which had been formed as a protest group to combat the plume trade, began. Other groups followed, and finally such lands formed the nucleus of the proposed State Park in 1930. Continuing purchases by well-known prominent citizens of Florida resulted in the establishment of the Park.

It was, however, not until after the Second World War, during the presidency of Harry S. Truman that the area was declared a National Park, and thus it became the first and most important wetlands park in the world. Its importance stretches far beyond its place as the biggest wetlands reserve in the New World. The constant spread of development, the conflicting

interests of farmers, settlers, hoteliers and sportsmen, have created continual strife and the arguments have continued in the full glare of the world's gaze. In Asia, Australia, Africa and Europe, where wetland habitats are disappearing under the advancing tide of human populations, with their expanding needs, conservationists, government environmentalists and concerned scientists have looked to the Everglades Park for the answers to their own dilemmas.

Three feeding White Ibis are just coming into their mature white plumage. For their first year they are brown, and some of these feathers have not yet moulted from these young birds.

There is much to be learned. More land has been wasted, and the ecological balance of more regions ruined, by ill-advised draining schemes than by any other cause, other than the destruction of rain forests. The folly of these acts, committed in the name of progress, is exceeded in magnitude only by their costs. In Florida, over $500 million have been spent in establishing and reconciling the needs of the various groups of people with those of the Park. This expenditure exceeds the cost of separating the reclaimed lands of Holland from the sea.

Reubin O'D Askew, when he was Governor, said of the State: 'Florida is forever facing choices between trees and towers, creeks or canals, marshes or marinas, water or waste, beaches or barriers, sunshine or smog and greenlands or ghettos.' As this is the same choice which is being faced everywhere, the lessons, both good and bad, should surely be heeded, for these great schemes have been less than successful in attaining their objectives. The fact is that all wetlands' ecosystems are extremely fragile, complicated and little understood, and that of Florida is certainly no exception.

That the numbers of birds in south Florida were enormous cannot be in doubt, but, on close examination of the available information, it seems

Everglade swamps

Next page. Yellow-crowned Night Heron.

Florida's Great Blue Herons are slightly paler than more northern birds. Shy and retiring in most areas, some of them have learned to steal from fishermen and become quite tame.

likely that the figures of birds quoted in millions cannot be sustained, either for the 1800s or after the ravages of the plume-hunters and the partial recovery to their former glory in the 1930s.

The devastation wrought by the insatiable demands of the plume trade continued unabated until the 1920s, and was unquestionably enormous. It seems likely, however, that the reports of numbers of birds in colonies of wading birds, and indeed seabirds, throughout the world were somewhat exaggerated. These numbers were offered partly in an understandable eagerness to bring attention to a situation which was desperately serious, needed headline-making support, but was so little understood by a sceptical world that dramatization was necessary if it was to create the necessary impact. Whatever the actual number of birds was at the time, there is no doubt that the vast majority of them were wiped out by plume-hunters; nor is there any doubt that a recovery took place everywhere in the 1930s, because fortunately at that time habitat was not destroyed, and that this recovery was due largely to the efforts of the then newly established conservation bodies which flourish today.

The result of this well-meaning, but perhaps over-enthusiastic use of numbers has somewhat rebounded upon those who now seek to present the situation as it has developed since the Second World War. I have sought to show throughout this book that the really substantial decline in wetland avifauna, and indeed in that of many other habitats, has been most rapid within the years of industrial and social expansion since the World Wars, and

that this decline in most areas (the Atlantic seaboard of North America being a notable exception) is much steeper than at any time in history, and has been accelerating within the last decade.

Roseate Spoonbills are increasing in numbers not only in the Everglades but throughout Florida.

Thus, exact figures which are available in the Everglades since 1974 confirm a continuous decline since then. The present position is extremely serious and modern students now know that, even in the last ten years, the figures established by using population survey techniques tell the grimmest story of all.

Symbolic of the problem is the heavily stressed Wood Stork *Mycteria americana*. In the 1920s estimates of its numbers varied between 75 000 and 100 000 individuals in Florida. By the 1960s, however, surveys showed only 24 000 adults, but by 1975 the numbers were down to 12 000 adults: a fall of 50% in less than 15 years (National Audubon Society Research Report No. 7). In the Everglades Park, the decrease in numbers between 1967 and 1982 was 65% (South Florida Research Center).

The various crises in the Park are well documented. Some years of drought in the 1960s highlighted the need for water to be supplied from storage areas as a matter of right, and not, as was then the system, only after all other needs had been met. When this was understood, and a system of priorities established, it became clear that it was not necessary merely to supply water, which had previously been available naturally, and apparently on a random basis, but that it was also essential to supply it at the correct time of the year and in the correct place.

A young Purple Gallinule searches the lily ponds. When adult it will turn bright blue and is a most colourful bird.

The Tricolor Heron. Often called the Louisiana Heron, it is found all over the United States and in Central and South America, though it is not as common as the Little Blue Heron.

Most wading birds nest in areas where abundant food sources are available. Colonial nesters need a readily available food supply, in very large quantities, when young need to be fed. In winter, the population of wading birds is markedly increased by the arrival of birds from the northern and central states and from Canada. These birds come to Florida in early autumn and leave again in February or March. Other species migrate into south Florida to nest. Wood Storks arrive from the north to nest in winter and early spring, while Roseate Spoonbills *Platalea ajaja* come in probably from the south, particularly Cuba, to nest during the same period. A proportion of all species of the wading birds that also visit Florida nest there, though this does not apply to the American Bittern *Botaurus lentiginosus* or to most shorebirds.

While some birds nest in the winter, between November and February, others are spring nesters, from March until June. Birds in Florida Bay are usually winter nesters, as are large species inland, but smaller herons and White Ibises *Eudocimus albus* nest in the spring. Seasonal rainfall is the most important factor governing food supplies and, consequently, nesting. Wood Storks are tactile feeders and take large fish. To obtain large amounts easily during the period when they are feeding young, they require to breed at the time when water levels are falling, and thereby making prey easier to obtain. Ibises, on the other hand, feed only in areas of shallow water, irrespective of prey density. If there is a drought, many birds will disperse without nesting; these species include Anhingas *Anhinga anhinga*, Everglade Kites *Rostrhamus sociabilis* and cormorants, as well as herons, ibises and spoonbills.

Many other species are affected to some extent, but to understand their different needs is difficult, and the sheer diversity of species, habitat and food requirements make detailed study a most complex matter.

Certainly the function of wading birds within the Florida ecosystem, and particularly the impact of the 14 different species on the diverse fish community, is not fully understood. It is known from experiments carried out by Dr James Kushlan that a fish kill, brought about by a deficiency of oxygen as water levels fell, eliminated 93% of all but six out of 26 species of fish present. This contrasts with a mixed wading-bird predation on a pond where 75% of the available stock was consumed, with no bias towards any particular species; this clearly showed the beneficial interaction at this level in the interlocking food chain.

This Osprey lives on fish which it captures in its strong talons. It can be found all over the world in wetland areas, but is particularly common in the Everglades.

The areas of deep water within the sawgrass are in most instances the result of the behaviour of alligators. These creatures create the reservoirs in which fish, reptiles and amphibians congregate as the water level recedes, and in turn retain a nucleus of breeding stock for rebuilding numbers on the return of the rains.

The breeding avifauna consists of comparatively few species compared with other areas of the world. The major exception is the larger number of species of herons, egrets and bitterns than is usually found. In Florida 11 species breed, over a sixth of the world's heron species.

There is but one nesting representative of grebe, pelican, cormorant, anhinga, spoonbill and crane, and only two of ibis, gallinule and rail. One tern also nests here, although two others do so on the Dry Tortugas; and usually only one duck, one shorebird, and the monotypic Limpkin *Aramus guaruana*. Thirty or so species of waterbird are non-breeders (fewer than

Anhingas spread their wings to dry in the sun after diving for fish. They spear their prey with their pointed bills. Their habit of swimming with only their neck exposed gives them the name 'Snake Bird'.

Double Crested Cormorants suffered badly when pesticides were commonly used, but have quickly recovered their numbers.

The Willet looks a very unprepossessing brown bird until it opens its wings to reveal a flash of white. Its alarm call echoes across the water when disturbed.

120 waterbirds are found in all of Florida), and the total number of bird species, including landbirds, is only 310. Compared with other parts of America, the Florida peninsula has a paucity of species.

The Everglades, nevertheless, provide a unique opportunity to study wetland species of North America. From the Park headquarters, southwards to Flamingo at the edge of Florida Bay, numerous trails have been built enabling visitors to travel either by car, or by walking – often on raised walkways across the marsh and quite close to water holes. These areas usually contain a surprisingly large number of birds which continue their daily lives within close range of crowds of people, who can watch them without apparently disturbing them in any way. Indeed, such birds have become known as 'people watchers', a phenomenon of reserves and parks. Roger Tory Peterson, the living legend among birders, has wondered at the indifference of birds to people on America's west coast, and suggested that Monterey is the ultimate place for photographic opportunities for birders. Undoubtedly, in the east, the Anhinga trail in the Everglades is a similar spot, as demonstrated by the annual migration of both professional and amateur photographers to its walkways.

With the influx of winter migrants, the chances of seeing birds increase in November, but, as the marshes dry out, so these growing numbers congregate more and more in the water holes and ponds. At this time the specially built viewing areas along the Anhinga and other trails become ever more rewarding to visit, and reach probably a peak viewing time in early February.

In Florida Bay, boats can be hired to pass near the numerous keys dotted across the shallows, but tides and strong winds can make it hazardous to venture too far, and landing on the birds' nesting islands is forbidden. Shorelines, however, provide good opportunities to observe waders, and places near the main buildings at Flamingo contain numbers of Brown Pelicans *Pelecanus occidentalis*. Gulls of several species are present throughout the year, while further along the coast, in the turtle grass, numerous small shorebirds are easily approached quite near to the motel and service area.

To visit the western area of the Park, a car journey down the Tamiami trail to Shark Valley is necessary. Along this road there are often large aggregations of feeding birds of many species, including White Ibises sometimes in flocks of many thousands. Across the canal which runs parallel to the road, the Everglade Kite can often be seen. Once in the Park, at Shark Valley, an open bus with a guide travels down across the sawgrass plain in a wide loop through the open glades to a large observation tower which looks right out towards the sea coast. Here is undoubtedly the best place to see alligators, and turtles, often sharing a rock with a Green Heron *Butorides striatus virescens*. The Green Heron is found both along the seashore and inland; nearly every pond and small stretch of water contains a pair.

The smaller Least Bittern *Ixobrychus exilis* is much more difficult to see and skulks in the reeds, though it is equally common throughout the Park. Its larger relation the American Bittern, unlike its European relative, does

The Bald Eagle still nests in Florida, but is much less common than it used to be. Its main diet is fish, but it has been known to kill and eat herons and other water birds.

not hide itself away, and during winter can often be seen in quite a small patch of reed.

While all the heron species have developed to fill different ecological niches, the most specialized is the Reddish Egret *Egretta rufescens*, which feeds on small fish in shallow estuarine habitats. To catch them it has adopted a dashing style, and turns and twists with wings half raised and crest erect. It has both a dark and a white morph, but interbreeding between the two colour forms does not produce multicolour young. Scientists have puzzled over the question of whether dark or white colouring gives the greater advantage for coastal feeding, but no very convincing proof of the advantage of one colour over the other has yet been advanced. Occupying a similar niche in the Far East, Swinhoe's Egret *E. eulophotes* has no dark colour phase, though the similar and more widespread Eastern Reef Heron *E. sacra* has.

Tricolor or Louisiana Herons *E. tricolor* dash after prey or walk slowly, as conditions dictate, and they will sometimes feed alongside other species such as the Pied-billed Grebe *Podilymbus podiceps*, whose dive disturbs prey normally out of their reach. Little Blue Herons *E. caerulea* are cautious feeders, but are equally at home in both salt and fresh water. The first-year birds of this species, however, are all-white, which causes confusion and adds to the difficulty of understanding the benefits that undoubtedly arise from this change of colour. One wonders if the Little Blue Heron is in the middle of an evolutionary change.

Of all the white species, the small Snowy Egret *E. thula* with its promi-

Brown Pelicans, like Cormorants, suffered badly during the period when pesticides were widely used. They have recovered their numbers now. To see them dive headlong onto the sea is a spectacular sight. Sometimes some of the fish they catch in their large pouches hang out from their bills and Laughing and other gulls will land on their backs and snatch the fish from them before they can be swallowed.

nent yellow feet seems to fill the same niche in Florida as the Little Egret *E. garzetta* does in the rest of the world, but this may be deceptive, and the position of white egrets taxonomically needs careful study on a wider basis than has hitherto been accepted. It needs to be based on a study of comparative behavioural patterns throughout the world. This applies even more to the Great White Egret *E. alba*, which is being classified variously as a monotypic genus 'Casmerodius' or by some workers as a true heron; studies of the other races of this species around the world, which have not been attempted professionally, will undoubtedly produce a rethink of this taxonomic position. Such studies may even suggest one day that convergent evolution has produced white egrets of apparent similarity, which may be found with increased study and knowledge to be of wholly different lineage.

The evolution of a completely white true heron *Ardea herodias occidentalis*, now acknowledged to be a race of the Great Blue Heron *A. herodias* and confined to a narrow area of the Caribbean and Florida coasts, may provide a key to the evolution of white and dark morphs. It may also reawaken the interest of the ornithological establishment in the study of geographical variations by fieldworkers, which may prove to be more rewarding than has hitherto been accepted.

Some ornithologists have suggested that white is less visible to fish than a darker colour. Fish-eating eagles add some credence to this theory. In Florida the Bald Eagle *Haliaeetus leucocephalus*, reduced so severely in numbers throughout its former range, has a white head and neck markedly similar to those of other eagles of the same genus such as African Fish Eagle

The Little Blue Heron feeds in both fresh and salt water and its range extends into most of South America. In its first year it is uniquely all white and it does not acquire its purple head and all blue wings and body until it is three years old. But it always has a black tip to its bill.

Turkey Vulture, a formidable raider and scavenger within the heronries.

H. vocifer and others. The Pallas's Fish Eagle *H. leucoryphus*, however, has a somewhat dirtier-coloured head and neck – perhaps indicating that it fishes in less clear waters!

The other common fish-eating bird of prey is the Osprey *Pandion haliaetus*, and it just holds its own here in the Everglades, as it does elsewhere around the world wherever it is not persecuted. Other competitors for the abundant fish stocks of Florida Bay include the highdiving Brown Pelican, the shallow-diving Double-crested Cormorant *Phalacrocorax auritus* and the fish-spearing Anhinga. Every other post and buoy in the bay seems to be a perch for one of these species, and when they are not in use they are occupied by one of the terns that winter or breed here.

Of the large wading birds that feed by touch, the White Ibis is the most numerous, and its will-o'-the-wisp relative, the Glossy Ibis *Plegadis falcinellus*, the rarest. The closely related Roseate Spoonbill has increased in numbers recently and must be counted as one of the success stories of the Park.

Of the numerous duck species found here in the winter, only the Mottled Duck *Anas fulvigula* stays to nest, and the Black-necked Stilt *Himantopus mexicanus* is the sole shorebird that regularly nests in the Park. Similarly, the Laughing Gull *Larus atricilla* and the Least (or Little) Tern *Sterna albifrons* are the only two seabirds to stay all the year round.

That three million people can live in the vicinity of the great wetlands park, and that hundreds of thousands of visitors come every year, is a remarkable achievement. There seems every reason to be optimistic about its prosperity if the future is faced with realism.

The fast-moving Sanderlings probe for food on the coast, running rapidly from place to place and dodging the incoming waves.

Reddish Egret. This is America's rarest heron.

2 South America

Northern Argentina

With a few exceptions, the birdlife of southern South America has been largely ignored until recent years, by both its inhabitants and its visitors alike.

The most notable of these exceptions is W H Hudson, who, though an Englishman, was born on the pampas of the Argentine. Present-day ornithologists in this country revere his name and works, which have pride of place in their club in Buenos Aires. Yet, when he left to come to Europe, the plume trade was at its height, and the 'myriads' of birds on the rivers and marshes, seen like clouds in the air, were gone or rapidly going. 'I hate the land of my birth', he wrote, 'and the Italian immigration that was blighting it' – though he later accepted that extermination was, at that time, a world-wide madness.

The exploitation of the natural resources of Argentina known as 'frutas de pais' has continued since early colonial days, but curiously the birdlife of this vast country stands comparison with that of any in the world, both in numbers and in variety of species, in spite of the devastation of the 1800s.

But times are changing here as elsewhere, with the political and economic expectations of the rapidly expanding population now being brought to fever pitch in this huge troubled country, and there are now plans

In the Chaco, there are more trees than in Corrientes and there is a wealth of small birds.

to develop and exploit the natural resources even of its more sparsely populated regions.

In the last decade, during a number of visits to the Argentine, I have been able to travel in the province of Buenos Aires, across the endless expanse of the pampas grazed by countless herds of cattle, to isolated swamps where the tall reed-beds hide the elusive Cocoi Heron *Ardea cocoi*; here they nest alongside their main predator, the Crested Caracara *Polyborus plancus*. I have visited the small clusters of farm buildings, which are shaded by stands of eucalyptus trees containing nests of the colonial-breeding Chimango Caracaras *Milvago chimango* and Monk Parakeets *Myiopsitta monachus*.

I have travelled northwards, too, into the province of Cordoba, for mile after mile along farm roads enclosed by never-ending picket fences, and on every other post a Burrowing Owl *Speotyto cunicularia* sat. By the water holes, where horses and cattle drank, were White-faced Glossy Ibises *Plegadis chihi*, a common species here, which feeds in large flocks in company with Brown-headed Gulls *Larus maculipennis* on the ploughed fields and pasture lands. Brown-streaked immature Night Herons *Nycticorax nycticorax* and screeching Southern Lapwings *Vanellus chilensis*, and the ever-present Chimangos, made up a strange mixture of unfamiliar birds.

These flat, open lands in Argentina with herds of hoofed animals seemed an ideal habitat for Cattle Egrets *Bubulcus ibis*, which anywhere else in such tropical conditions would have been seen in abundance. But the commonest of the heron family proved to be the Whistling Heron *Syrigma sibilatrix*,

A Rufescent Tiger Heron on its large stick nest high in the trees above the open marshland. One white downed chick sits along side an addled egg. Only remnant forest remains in this area, but the large heron is quite common here and not at all shy.

The Southern Lapwing has a red spur on its wing. It is a noisy bird which screeches loudly at every intrusion upon its territory.

This Buff-necked Ibis is one of the commonest of the many species of Ibis found in South America.

though it did not stray too far from trees, which appear to be its invariable roosting place. It has spread widely, and, whereas it was a summer migrant in W H Hudson's day, when he looked forward to its return each spring, it can now be found at all seasons of the year all over the country.

In the mid 1970s, I had made one brief visit to the north of the country, to the province of Chaco, and found there a wealth of birdlife which appeared to have been hitherto unrecorded in any detail. I was therefore encouraged, together with a team of colleagues from Britain and the United States, to pay a longer visit to investigate this ornithologically little-known area. This was made easier by the offer of hospitality from the great industrial and ranching consortium of Arbol Solo, and by the request from the government of the Chaco region for us to make an assessment of the potential for, and ecological consequences of, both irrigating the dry areas and creating dams on the Parana, thus lowering the water table in the wetland areas of this province. While having no intention of halting their grandiose plans, they were very conscious of the disastrous effects caused by the wholesale destruction by developers in the Amazon basin and the Mato

Grosso regions of their neighbour Brazil to the north.

The two rivers, the Parana with its headwaters in the Brazilian highlands and the Paraguay fed by the swamplands of the Mato Grosso, join together and, in meeting, flow southwards between the two northern Argentine cities of Resistancia, the provincial capital of the Chaco, and Corrientes, the capital city of the province of that name. The combined waters of these silt-laden rivers form the River Plate and reach the sea at Buenos Aires, separating Argentina from Uruguay and its capital Montevideo on the northern bank of the wide estuary.

Resistancia is a typical farming community and has, like many of the towns serving the isolated ranches, a well-kept steam engine built in some northern English workshop to serve as a monument and a reminder of trade links with Britain long since severed and now perhaps unhappily beyond restoration. Reminders of India in the days of the British Raj remain, too. The Forrestal group erected low-roofed houses of the same design as and of similar materials to those used in the Indian dak bungalows. These were to house their farm managers during the period of exploitation of the exten-

The large South American Cocoi Heron has spectacular colourage in its courtship phase. It nests mainly in reed beds, unlike the Great Blue Heron, its relative in North America.

Southern Screamers are 'turkey-like' birds. They build huge nests in the reed beds and their calls echo across the pampas.

sive northern forests for timber and also for tannin from the quebracho *Aspidosperma quebracho blanco*. Tannin was used to cure the hides of the cattle, so that both beef and leather were exported.

We travelled by road through the Chaco regions. In the reed-filled ditches numbers of Snail Kites *Rostrhamus sociabilis* flew. They hunted in flocks, as their scientific name suggests, in marked contrast to the rarely glimpsed individuals of the same species which one sees in the Florida Everglades and there called Everglade Kites.

The diversity of habitat in the Argentinian Chaco, which is a vast province and comprises about half of the natural geographical region called the Gran Chaco, is very great, and contains a wide range of wet and dry regions, and thus an equally diverse avifauna. Remnants of gallery forest stretch along the Paraguay–Parana river, and bordering these are palm savannas in areas named 'pantanal', which are flooded for part of the year and where the water table is close to the surface. This wet grassland is scattered with groves of palm trees and dry woodland islands known as 'embalsados'. There are areas of permanent swamp and some small lakes, and these hold some wetland birds. It is evident, however, that such areas do

This young Whistling Heron in its full,
quite spectacular plumage. This
heron is found everywhere in the
Argentine.

The ground feeding Campos Flicker's wings match the trees bark pattern and is a relic species of the once extensive wet woodland areas which stretched across much of this part of the Argentine.

not support large numbers of wading birds. Although we saw White-faced Glossy Ibises and American Wood Storks *Mycteria americana* flying in tight formations overhead, and some birds feeding at the pools, there were no large flocks of egrets, but just a very few Snowy Egrets *Egretta thula* and the occasional small group of Great White Egrets *E. alba*. We saw no sign of nesting colonies throughout our journeys by car and later by light plane, and it was evident that large numbers of wading birds were not present.

The subtropical temperatures brought hot, humid days and nights, the thermometer showing 95°F. Occasionally the sky darkened and gales of near-hurricane force brought blinding rainstorms; only then did the

temperature fall. Flying was hazardous, and one such journey caused the pilot to weave his plane between huge dark and menacing clouds in his attempt to avoid the heavy turbulence on the edges of the gathering storm.

In the northern area of the dry Chaco, we were able to visit a lake reached by truck forced through thick, thorny scrub in the well-named region called 'El Impenetrable'. Here we found a wealth of wetland birds, including Buff-necked Ibis *Theristicus caudatus* and the rare dull brown Plumbeous Ibis *Harpiprion caerulescens*, as well as Roseate Spoonbills *Platalea agaga*. Two huge Jabiru Storks *Jubiru mycteria* dwarfed the many species of duck, of which over 300 Tinged Teal *Anas leucophrys* made up the largest flock, but there were smaller numbers of White-faced Ducks *Dendrocygna viduata* and Black-bellied Tree Ducks *D. autumnalis,* Muscovy Ducks *Cairina moschata,* Brazilian Teal *Amazonetta brasiliensis* and the delicately marked Rosy-billed Pochard *Netta peposaca*. Birds of prey were always in evidence in a country where birds are largely unmolested, and the species seen included Crane Hawk *Geranospiza caerulescens*, Great Black Hawk *Buteogallus urubitinga*, several Savanna Hawks *Heterospizias meridionalis* and a single Black-collared Hawk *Busarellus nigricollis*; Crested Caracaras were common, both in the wetlands and across the dry savanna. Some Greater Yellowlegs *Tringa melanoleuca* were wintering here, and the Smooth-billed Anis *Crotophaga ani*

Great White Egrets range across the wetland areas. They are rare birds in this region of the Argentine and we saw no sign of nesting colonies.

Whistling Herons are not usually colonial breeders. This single small stick nest holds two fully grown young. A tropical storm the day before had blown the third young to the ground and we found it lying dead beneath the tree. There are not enough tree nesting sites for colonial breeding birds in this area of Corrientes.

Next page.
Above. Black Vultures looking for a meal.
Below. Limpkin. This long-legged marsh bird is the only member of its family. It lives on fresh water snails and reptiles.

(a member of the cuckoo family), found as far north as the Florida Everglades, formed clusters of noisy family parties around the lakeside trees.

On leaving the Chaco and crossing the river into Corrientes, we flew across extensive areas of pantanal which had some quite large 'esteros'. These marshy lakes had noisy families of the well-named Southern Screamer *Cheauna torquata*, which stretched their turkey-like necks in angry rebuke at our intrusion. Great numbers of capybaras *Hydrochoerus hydrochaeris*, the world's largest rodent, moved in herds through the open lake waters, and around the edges of the lake were rails of several species.

Limpkins *Aramus guarauna* and gallinules of three species – Common *Gallinula chloropus*, Purple *Porphyrula martinica* and Spot-flanked Porphyriops melanops – had fledged young, and we spotted a White-winged Coot *Fulica leucoptera* and glimpsed a Giant Wood Rail *Aramides ypecaha*.

The Cocoi Heron appeared briefly in the distance from time to time, in contrast with the frequent appearances of the Whistling Heron, which was encountered in all types of habitat and which we found to be a semi-colonial feeder and a species that invariably gathered in numbers to roost each evening. Much more difficult was the task of finding its nest; when, after much searching and enquiring of the local people, one containing young was discovered, it was a single nest in an isolated tree far out across the open pampas, on the Santa Barbara ranch in Corrientes.

One of the difficulties we discovered in asking for details of the Whistling Heron locally was that it was not considered by the country people to be a heron: they called it 'Chiflon', not 'Garza' (which is the Spanish for 'heron'). As we observed it more regularly, such distinction became clear, for in flight the wings do not travel above the horizontal and so it has the flight charac-

Plush-capped Jay.

teristics of a duck; to add to the analogy, the fledged young whistle like geese, and the musical flute-like call of the adults proclaims its name 'The Whistler'. It is only some 20 years since taxonomists placed this unusual and hitherto almost unknown heron in the night heron group, so that our observations were of special interest.

The lack of egret numbers was compensated for by the diversity of other unfamiliar species. Tiger herons, glimpsed briefly by ornithologists in the isolated pockets of distribution in New Guinea, West Africa and Central America, were seen regularly once located in the marshlands and stands of trees in Corrientes, and the Rufescent Tiger Heron *Tigrisoma lineatum* appears to be a quite abundant bird and far from crepuscular in its habits. It may be that its appearance in the open at this time of year was due to its breeding activities. Certainly, our exciting discovery of a nest 24 feet (7.5 m) up in a tree within a few hundred yards of the ranchhouse in which we were living dispelled the view that it was a shy, retiring species. The nest contained a newly hatched chick and an unhatched egg of white, blotched with red at one end. Constant observation showed that only at night was the chick fed, and then only once.

Our building of a hide in a neighbouring tree overlooking the nest was watched by the adult birds; they stayed quite close, and settled happily to shade the young from the strong sun as soon as the hide was closed and we were in position for photography. The resultant pictures are to date unique,

Snowy Egret. The plumes and bright
soft colors are used aggressively
quite regularly away from the nest
much more often than other egrets.

and it was unfortunate that shortage of time precluded us from continuing to obtain further pictures of this little-known, but evidently far from rare species.

We erected mistnets in the wooded areas throughout our journeys in the Chaco and in Corrientes, and the checklist details a host of species which tested to the full the combined knowledge of the ornithologists from Britain, America and the Argentine, represented by, respectively: Dr Christopher Perrins of the Edward Grey Institute of Field Ornithology, Oxford; John Ogden of the National Audubon Research Department, Florida, USA; and Dr Claudio Blanco of the Direccion Nacional de Fauna Silvestre, Buenos Aires, Argentina.

In 1980, when our main expedition took place, we had high hopes of returning. The fragile ecosystems we were privileged briefly to see required much more detailed research. Our concern was unanimous: wholesale drainage schemes, diverting of rivers, parcelling out of land for peasant farming had not been assessed with any understanding of the complexity of the problems to be faced.

Much careful scientific study is required if here, as elsewhere in the world, the whole balance of the ecosystem is not to be irrevocably damaged by ill-considered schemes. The story is all too familiar and, without such care, wetland areas will disappear, taking with them still undiscovered wildlife.

Recent political events have prevented continued study of a region rich in species, but perhaps lack of capital resources in the immediate short term will give a breathing space to this threatened environment, giving wiser counsel an opportunity to prevent complete destruction on the scale being witnessed elsewhere in South America.

3 Africa

The Tana River, Kenya

On the lower reaches of the Tana River, as indeed on almost its whole length, the riverine forest has long since been destroyed, giving way to banana trees and millet and maize crops, planted to the river's edge. The ensuing heavy soil erosion has turned the fast-flowing river into a dull brown carrier of silt to its mouth, in Formosa Bay, south of Lamu on the shores of the Indian Ocean.

The Tana's source is the series of mountain streams from the Aberdare Mountain Range; as it turns northwards, it also receives the rivulets from mount Kenya. Thus, in addition to melting snows, the forest rains combine with annual rains of the coastal belt to swell the waters as the river bends southwards to the sea, overflowing into the inundated areas, filling the lakes and ponds and creating rich marshlands, which produce an abundant food supply for waterbirds of all types.

South of Garsen, one of these annually or, occasionally, bi-annually flooded lakes is a traditional breeding site for herons and other large waterbirds. This colony is normally active during the long rains of April and May,

Egyptian Geese are a common sight around water-holes in Africa.

The huge stately Saddle-billed Stork has a distinctive black and red bill. Though mainly a fish eater, it will eat small mammals and birds as well as reptiles. These birds pair for life.

and, additionally, some species such as the Open-billed Stork *Anastomus lamelligerus* nest here during the short rains, when their main food, snails of the *Pila* species, emerge from aestivation in the many ponds, ditches and shallow lakes. Should the rains fail, such food species will remain in a state of torpor and nesting will not take place.

The year 1982 was exceptional. Mean annual rainfall for the coastal region, including the lower Tana, shows April and May to be the peak months, with 16.24 and 25.23 mm respectively, whereas the short rains in October and November amount to less than half this (source: Kenya Meteorological Department, in Brown and Britten 1979). In 1982,

The Intermediate Egret is called the Yellow-billed Egret in Africa. It is halfway in size between the Little and the Great Egret. On the Tana River it was shier than the other two herons.

however, October brought the heaviest rains since 1961; these were widespread through Kenya, and continued intermittently until January.

The area in January 1983 presented a picture of thick vegetation clogging the borders of well-filled lakes and ponds. Around the riverside villages, catch crops of rice planted along the mud edges of the inundated areas were well grown, and tall grass grew in the usually dry acacia woodlands. Among the flowering water-lilies *Nymphaea* spp., flocks of up to 150 Open-billed Storks found snails plentiful. Marabou Storks *Leptoptilos crumeniferus*, the village scavengers, were fishing; Yellow-billed Storks *Mycteria ibis* flew in brightly coloured parties of ten or more birds.

To get to the traditional heronry was unusually difficult. A strong current down the main river enabled us to make a fast journey by dugout canoe to the borders of the lake, but tangled mangrove barred the access to the lake, which was unapproachable from any other direction because of the deep marshy swamp. Once on the lake, the water was heavily covered with thick tall rhizomatous grass *Echinocloa stagnina*.

In the clumps of bushes *Combretum constructum* and the trees *Terminalia brevipes*, which rose some 15 feet (4.6 m) above the water, the heronry was fully active, but on closer inspection proved to be very differently populated from the composition in the main season. The dominant species was the Yellow-billed Egret *Egretta intermedia brachyhyncha*, which made up as much as half of the nesting population of herons, and these were side by side

Exotic water lilies flower around the reed-beds at the Tana River heronry.

with Purple Herons *Ardea purpurea* which had, for reasons not readily apparent, abandoned their traditional reed sites for places high up in the canopy of bushes. Numerous Squacco Herons *Ardeola ralloides*, some in full nuptial plumes and others still in streaky non-breeding dress, appeared to be in the early stages of egg-laying, while the few Night Herons *Nycticorax nycticorax* had half-grown young sharing the bare branches above their nests with equally well-grown Purple Heron chicks.

Of the other herons there was little to be seen. Close examination revealed a few Black Herons *Egretta ardesiaca* deep in the bush foliage, tightly sitting, presumably on eggs. A few Little Egrets *E. garzetta* standing by nests had blue-grey lores, indicating that they had finished their courtship displays; the bright red lores used in these ceremonies had faded when the first eggs were laid. Fewer still were the Great White Egrets *E. alba melanorhynchos*, and no individuals with bright coloured 'soft parts' were seen. An occasional Grey Heron *Ardea cinerea* flew overhead, brightly plumed and with a dark-patterned shiny neck. These were probably nesting well back in the colony. Not so the Cattle Egrets *Bubulcus ibis*: busy, tightly packed parties of ten or so birds flew low over the water on our way down the river, but within the nesting area only an occasional buff-coloured bird could be seen. In high season this abundant, terrestrial feeding bird is often the earliest nest-builder, and the rains trigger off its aggressive, highly active breeding, timed fully to exploit amphibian abundance. It was evident that not many were breeding and it seemed likely that they would not now do so despite being present in the area in large numbers.

Purple Herons will nest either in reed beds or in trees amongst the other colonial nesting birds. Here on the Tana River they will change from one breeding site to another according to the season.

Top left. All over Kenya the laughing call of the Hadada Ibis can be heard as it flies from one stretch of water to another. A confiding bird, it is the commonest ibis throughout much of the African continent.

Bottom left. Ground Hornbills feed both on the dry savanna and in flooded wetland areas where they eat crabs and frogs. They nest in large hollow trees.

A pair of Crowned Cranes feed on the grass seeds which ripen as the marshland dries out.

The numbers of Cattle Egrets discovered in the following June reinforced the impression that this short-rains nesting activity had not altered their annual abundant nesting at their usual time of breeding – after the long rains. Around our camp site, small parties had come to feed from first light and herds of goats and cattle all had their attendant flocks, but few of these birds had developed the bright buff plumes and the deep yellow legs which indicate readiness to breed.

It is irresistible to postulate that this was a chance for the less aggressive species to succeed without the fierce competition of the more dominant species. Undoubtedly, the Purple Herons had begun a secondary breeding cycle, perhaps through failure in the main season. Erratic, shy, and not breeding regularly, this specialized heron has a long rear toe adapted for life among the reeds, where the nominate race, at least, usually nest, though in Asia this is less commonly so. Apart from a small number of Night Herons, with their habit of stealing both eggs and young from their neighbours, this true heron species seemed to have had the site to itself for several weeks before being joined by Yellow-billed Egrets. Internationally called Intermediate Egret, this species has, unlike its congeners, the habit of easily abandoning nesting if conditions are not right, or at least of building later

than its fellow egrets, perhaps to avoid aggressive competition. At any rate, perhaps 50% of the birds nesting were of this shorter Yellow-billed Egret.

The relationship between the Yellow-billed Egret and the so-called Plumed Egret *E. i. plumifera* of Australia is very close. Both are identical in all phases of plumage and soft-part coloration, and their average wing measurements overlap (though accepting the mean to be somewhat larger among the African birds); this seems to imply that the races are inseparable and should be merged. The nominate race of Asia, however, is a different matter entirely and could conceivably prove to be different at species level.

While other colonial waterbird species can, and do, nest in groups of their own, they seem to prosper better with a mixed assemblage, and this out-of-season colony was no exception. The African Darter *Anhinga rufa* was actively feeding growing chicks, but the few Sacred Ibises *Threskiornis aethiopicus* and the unpredictable Glossy Ibises are even more temperamental than other ibis species, and, whereas the conservative heron species use traditional sites year after year, these cosmopolitan birds seldom nest to any regular or foreseeable pattern. Long-tailed Cormorants *Phalacrocorax africanus*, and the few larger Common Cormorants *P. carbo*,

The Long-toed Lapwing has feet designed for walking on floating vegetation.

The Black Heron is the only member
of its family that forms a complete
umbrella over its head. Whether this
is to attract fish to its shade or in
order that it can see more easily is
not known. This photograph captures
the fish at the point of being speared
which is achieved with a downward
vertical thrust of the bill.

are always attracted to existing colonies and, although many just lounge on the sidelines, many others were actively building. African Spoonbills *Platalea alba* had come, too, building close to each other in tightly packed groups, surrounded by other species. All had the bright red flash of early courtship to their legs and it seemed eggs were about to be laid, after which the flash would gradually subside. Certainly the stick-carrying ceremonies of early ritualistic courtships were over.

The one species which was spread through the colony in considerable numbers was the Open-billed Stork. This probably nested most regularly at this usually off-season period, and birds were arriving laden with weed dredged up from the bottom of the lake to form a lining for their stick nests. January breeding had been previously reported from this area, and there seemed little doubt that the dominant factor behind the arrival of this wide-ranging stork was the breeding cycle of the particular snail species which was so abundant here.

On the river, Green Herons *Butorides striatus atricapillus* flitted across the water; often named the 'Mangrove Heron', they had their own nest sites away from the colony. The large Saddle-billed Stork *Ephippiorhynchus sene-galensis* is widespread but nowhere common in Kenya; a few pairs annually at Amboseli and in the Masai Mara. The rarer Woolly-necked Stork *Ciconia episcopus* inhabited the mangrove of the coral shore around Mombasa to the south of Formosa Bay, and the dark-phased Western Reef Herons *Egretta gularis* had already started to build among the few bushes on Kisite Island, flighting in from neighbouring reefs as the tide flowed.

Jet black Open-billed Storks gather snails among the lilies. These storks wander across the continent in search of large snails and other crustaceans. Large flocks gather to feed and then move on to other areas when the food supply is finished.

The Blacksmith Plover lays its eggs in a scrape by the water's edge and seems to spend most of its time warding off, sometimes quite huge mammals, as they come down to drink.

The Black-headed Heron feeds in open dry pasture on insects but also around water holes when it consumes all manner of reptiles and small mammals.

The unresolved controversy over this reef heron and its relationship with the Little Egret *E. garzetta* is discussed in *The Herons of the World* (1978), and argument persists. The former's bright yellow lores, present in both dark and white phases, suggest that this colony on Kisite Island is the Indian Ocean race *dimorpha*. On Lake Turkana dark-plumed birds of the race *schistacea* are present in a Little Egret colony on Bird Island and appear to mate with them. Evidence from India strongly supports the view that such interbreeding occurs regularly and that all Western Reef Herons at least of the race *schistacea* must be considered as Little Egret forms.

The heavy rains had stimulated thick lakeshore vegetation, thus depriving wintering Palearctic waders of mudflats on which to feed, but near to the sea coast most of the species wintered or passed through at various stages of the Eurasian winter. The heavy vegetation did provide suitable habitat for the delicate, high-stepping Long-toed Plover *Vanellus crassirostris*, which, like the abundant Jacanas *Actophilornis africanus*, walk across the floating grasses and lily leaves.

This area of east Kenya is becoming more heavily populated, and wild animals are scarcer now than even ten years ago. Long grass after the rains

Little Egrets have yellow feet and, as with this bird, they loose their breeding plumage well before their young leave the nest. Their lores too, turn gradually back to blue-grey.

Next page. African Fish Eagle.

The Tana River Colony has many different species nesting in the trees around the marsh.

Previous page. A Pied Kingfisher.

does, however, provide cover for the small feline hunter of birds, the serval *Felis serval*. Its long legs are used to aid its sight in such cover, and, unlike other predators, it can detect ground-nesting birds by means of its large ears, rather than by scent. Around the heronry, crocodiles provide a sanitation function, as do vultures and Marabou Storks.

There is a strong case for efficient protection of this important but little-known breeding area for many of Africa's spectacular waterbirds before it is overtaken by population expansions and drainage schemes.

4 India

Bharatpur

In summer the heat of India is no 'Asian solar myth'. From the foothills of the Himalayas to the central plains, the sun scorches down. Only when the monsoon rains come is there some relief, and it is then that the famous Keoladeo National Bird Sanctuary springs to life. Starting quietly but gradually erupting into a blaze of colourful activity, the most spectacular heronry in Asia plays host to thousands of herons, ibises, spoonbills, storks, cormorants, darters and small species of endless variety. The trees and reed-beds are filled with nests and the aquatic life teems in the artificially flooded lagoons, providing immense quantities of food for the breeding birds.

By September, in addition to this great spectacle, the cooler weather brings the arrival of the winter migrants. Ducks, geese, coots, eagles, cranes, waders and a host of small birds fly south from as far north as western Siberia. Birds that have nested in the arctic tundra, across the flood plains of the River Ob west of the Ural Mountains, along the shores of the Caspian Sea, east to longitude 120°, travel southwards across Afghanistan, funnelling through the northern passes into Pakistan and on down the Indus river to fan out across the Indian sub-continent.

The centuries-old migration was exploited by early Asian man, who learnt to trap, net and in more recent times to shoot these winter visitors. Ducks found food in the jheels, in the river valleys and in the inundated marshlands of northern India, and congregated in huge numbers.

Bharatpur

In the late 1800s, the then Maharajah of Bharatpur visited England and was entertained at shooting parties. This experience stimulated him to create a duck preserve, and he developed and improved the natural winter habitat of the wetland birds so that very large concentrations of waterfowl could be shot by leading sportsmen of the day. In quite a small area he built a honeycomb of raised earth embankments, wide enough to carry carts. With the aid of sluices between the bunds, the level of water in the resultant artificially created lakes and swampy marshlands can be controlled. This depends upon rain falling during the monsoon, but

additional water comes along a canal, which is part of the wider Ajan Bund irrigation scheme fed from the Banganga and Gambhir rivers; in years when the monsoon rains fail, this system provides the only source of water.

Bharatpur was an independent state of great power under Saraj Mal, with 'Jat Ulysses', and, though its power declined, the quarrelsome Jats were, and are, fine farmers. They cultivated the rich Punjab lands, and were able to bring to the task of irrigation at Bharatpur the accumulated knowledge of centuries. It is this inherited ability to manipulate the delicate water balance that has brought about the success of this wetlands preserve, and sets it apart from other more grandiose schemes that have failed for lack of such expertise.

In 1902, when the original scheme was completed, Lord Curzon, the Viceroy of India, was the first important guest to shoot at Bharatpur, but in 1938 the then Viceroy, Lord Linlithgow, and his party surpassed all records by slaughtering 4 273 birds in a day. The Second World War brought many famous military leaders here, and the sight of the flat-topped camel carts piled high with birds after continuous and concentrated firing turned many who witnessed it, including myself, against this form of mass execution.

The ingenious system of signals by strategically placed beaters enabled the flocks of ducks and geese to be moved in sequence from different parts of the preserve over the guns again and again, so that the sky was filled with birds continuously for several hours. Each member of the party kept a loader busy reloading and cooling his second gun while he fired with the

Open-billed Storks of Asia are all grey compared with their all black African relatives. They are among the first birds to start nesting as the heronry springs to life at the start of the monsoon rains.

The majestic Imperial Eagle is, unlike the Golden Eagle, a bird of the open plains. Across central and Eastern Europe it has become very rare and it is unusual to see more than one or two of these magnificent birds in Bharatpur.

The Red-Wattled Lapwing is a common bird everywhere in India. Some even nest around the lawns of the Maharaja's palace, and their shrill cries echo across the reserve at the dusk and dawn.

first. Many birds were wounded, and firing was temporarily halted from time to time while dogs and men were sent into the water, the reed-beds and tangled bushes to retrieve winged birds. What had been a day's sport had become an unacceptable travesty and the tide of opinion moved inexorably against such excesses. The last shoot was held in 1954.

By 1956 the preserve had become a bird sanctuary of some 29 km², of which 11 are inundated to a depth of up to 1.7 m by the monsoon rains, and aided by the water channelled from the Ajan dam. In 1981 the sanctuary was declared a National Park, and in 1982 all grazing of cattle and the right of way of villagers through the reserve was stopped.

This action was, of course, extremely controversial, for the villagers around the reserve had come to depend upon the ample grazing to build up their herds of cattle and buffalo. The people, too, were aggressive in their attacks on the concept of restricting their access to the land. The resultant clash was inevitable, and bloodshed resulted when the Forest Guards enforced the new restrictions.

The results, however, have shown a marked change in the chances of survival of this refuge of international importance. Within such a small area the constant intrusion on an ever-increasing scale was destroying the sanctuary. With proper management and careful scientific scrutiny, however, this microcosm of former extensive wetlands of Asia now has a good chance of survival. There is a danger, however, that extensive growth of the marsh grass *Paspalum distichum*, previously kept in check by the water buffalo, could prove a major problem. Some method must be found to keep free the rapidly clogging waterways. Problems constantly arise in man-managed reserves, emphasizing the need for close monitoring to ensure that the ecological balance is not upset.

The importance of preserving this wetland sanctuary cannot be over-emphasized. Over 360 species of birds have been recorded from here. The huge concentrations of some of these are amazing. Here is an area where

This spoonbill has fully grown young at its nest. When they fly some birds will make the long journey to winter on the shores of the Caspian sea. Others will spend the winter here in India.

quite close observations can be made, not only in the study of behaviour and identifications of species, but in the interaction between these species.

The seasonal movement of birds to and from Bharatpur is well documented. Behind the concept of creating the reserve, the driving force had been India's leading ornithologist, Dr Sálim Ali. This world figure not only brought his personal influence to bear in establishing and managing this park, during the period between 1963 and 1974, but he led a team of

The numbers of Painted Storks are greater here than anywhere else in Asia.

five professional and nine amateur ornithologists who ringed no fewer than 72 577 birds of 224 different species. This prodigious effort formed part of the extensive programme of the Migratory Animal Pathological Survey (MAPS), which was organized by Dr Elliott McClure and which established and funded ringing stations throughout Asia with the sole and unfortunate exception of mainland China, which could not join for political reasons.

In spite of this exclusion, the knowledge of the movement of birds across the continents has been enormously enhanced by this work, and the importance of Bharatpur as a wintering ground for migrants has become startlingly clear. Recent work, too, in the Upper Indus valley near the village of Titse in central Ladakh, by a group from England's Southampton University, has shown interesting movements of birds across the Himalayas. While species such as Coots *Fulica atra*, many ducks, geese, birds of prey, and smaller species are exclusively migrants, it has been established that a proportion of birds that have resident populations in India also migrate. Some Spoonbills *Platalea leucorodia* nest on the Caspian Sea, and there is a detectable movement northwards of several species of heron in spring.

Inevitably, attention is drawn to the special rarity in India, the Siberian White Crane *Grus leucogeranus*. This majestic white crane now winters again in Bharatpur and adds another dimension to conservation here. Like the Whooping Crane *G. americana*, this specialized migratory species totters dangerously near the edge of extinction. Fewer than 200 individuals have

been counted in the wild in recent years. Only two widely separated breeding areas still remain and it is from the more westerly of these, on the marshlands of the Ob river delta in northern USSR, that birds travel south to winter at Bharatpur. A small proportion of this breeding population travels across to the Volga delta and southwards to Feredonkener in Iran, but the majority, perhaps some 30 to 40 birds, travel due south, stopping en route at Ab i Etadu in Afghanistan, and then onwards across the Himalayan mountains. They then travel down the Kurram valley in Pakistan to follow the Indus river, and arrive at the reserve to winter from November until March.

This journey is hazardous in the extreme. If they survive the journey to

The Painted Stork brings sticks to its nest. It is much more aggressive than the much smaller Open-bill and will often drive it from its nest site.

Pallas's Fish Eagle is present in Bharatpur and a pair usually nests here. Unusually for a bird of prey it stays here all year round.

The Lesser Spotted Eagle winters in India. Adult birds lose their spots and are hard to distinguish from the Greater Spotted Eagles, some of which also arrive here to over winter.

Buff colouring on the Oriental White Ibis distinguishes it from the Sacred Ibis of Africa.

the Indian sub-continent, they are forced along Pakistan's Northwest Frontier, where between 1000 and 1500 professional crane-trappers trap or shoot Common *G. grus* or Demoiselle Cranes *Anthropoides virgo* as well as the highly valued Siberian White Crane. These are men of the Wazir and Mahsud tribes, whom the British attempted to hold in check along the Durrant line, which terminated in the walled fort at Tazmak at the head of the valley. When I was stationed there in the early 1940s it housed six battalions of troops, who found the task of keeping law and order a challenging one. There is thus no hope of enforcing conservation laws upon such wild tribesmen, even supposing Pakistan had such regulations, which, unlike India, it has not yet introduced.

While the pressures on migration are increasing for all species making the journeys, equal pressures are mounting in the breeding areas. Development of farming and widespread industrialization has brought increasing threats to the previously unexploited lands of Siberia, and the steady march of urbanization eastwards from the Urals constantly reduces the undisturbed habitats of former years.

These breeding-ground pressures upon migrants highlight the need to provide a safe, secure winter haven in this, the most strategically placed wintering ground for central Palearctic species. Elsewhere it can be seen that at the eastern end of the Palearctic pressures are event greater, and nowhere more evident than in Japan (see Shinhama Reserve).

Breeding birds in the Keoladeo sanctuary, and particularly the large wading birds, need an abundant food supply and secure nesting sites. The occa-

The Great Cormorants have white faces here in Asia and are a separate race from those found in Europe. Their nests are built tightly packed together in parts of huge heronries.

sional failure of the monsoon rains does not greatly affect the reproduction of amphibians and fish; stocks quickly recover, as they did after the extremely dry season of 1979. Longer-term drought, however, not only destroys breeding stocks of all fish on a non-selective basis, but quickly kills the trees and water foliage and leads to deterioration of the whole ecosystem.

Babul *Acacia milotica* and Ber *Ziziphus mauritiana* are the most important and abundant species of tree for nesting birds, and the dense reed-beds provide additional sites for ground-nesting species. The cycle of wet and dry creates a level of salinity which assists in abundant and fast-growing aquatic life, and the whole delicate system thus established needs constant monitoring. Introduced species of vegetation, whether trees or the ubiquitous water hyacinth *Eichhornia*, which has clogged waterways from Brazil to Bali, upset the ecological balance and highlight the need for constant vigilance in what, of necessity, becomes an area requiring intensive scientific management.

The checklist for the Bharatpur (or Ghana) Reserve reveals a wide variety of wading birds. The heron species are particularly diverse. The Grey Heron *Ardea cinerea* and the reed-nesting Purple Heron *A. purpurea* are the two representatives of the true day heron family. Egrets of three species, Great White *Egretta alba*, Intermediate *E. intermedia* and Little *E. garzetta*, are abundant and give a unique opportunity to observe their different

behaviour and appearance. The Cattle Egret *Bubulcus ibis* is of the eastern race *coromandus*, and the Pond Heron *Ardeola grayii* is endemic to India. Night Herons *Nycticorax nycticorax* reflect their status as one of the commonest of the heron family, while no fewer than three bitterns make up a total of nine members of the Ardeidae.

The Asian Open-billed Stork *Anastomus oscitans* is the first to begin nesting, and the Painted Stork *Mycteria leucocephalus* the last to leave the colony in March. The white-necked *Ciconia episcopus* (called Woollynecked in Africa) and Black-necked Storks *Ephippiorhynchus asiaticus* are present in small numbers, while visitors include European White Storks *Ciconia ciconia* and, from southern India, the Adjutant *Leptoptilos dubius* and Lesser Adjutant Storks *L. javanicus*.

The Black-necked Stork builds a large solitary nest. It is rare now, except at the extremes of its extensive range in India at the west and in the swamplands of Australia at the east. This large-billed stork is extremely pugnacious and highly territorial in its feeding behaviour, harassing both herons and cranes should they intrude. The Oriental White Ibis *Threskiornis aethiopicus melanocephalus*, now classified as a subspecies of the Sacred Ibis, and the shy, erratic Glossy Ibis *Plegadis falcinellus* are colonial nesters, but the Black Ibis *Pseudibis papillosa* is, like the Black-necked Stork, a solitary species and somewhat unpredictable as to its choice of site for breeding, although it

The Indian Pond Heron are everywhere here but strangely do not nest in the reserve. Probably the competition from other species is too strong so they prefer to find a tree away from the colony.

Next page. The Siberian Crane travels from its breeding grounds in the Ob valley in northern Russia. Its hazardous route brings it across Afghanistan and down the Pakistan mountains to the Indus River. It is attacked all the way, and it is not surprising that ever fewer reach their traditional wintering grounds.

Indian Rollers perform spectacular courtship displays and roll and dive like fighter planes as they pair-bond prior to nesting.

Previous page. Intermediate Egret with young. This is the commonest white egret in Bharatpur.

always chooses a tall tree. Three species of pelican, Rosy *Pelecanus onocrotalus*, Dalmatian *P. crispus* and the commonest, Spot-billed or Grey *P. philippensis*, visit the reserve but do not nest. On the other hand, three cormorants and the sharpbilled Indian Darter *Anhinga rufa* do swell the colonial tree nesting assemblage.

Predators and scavengers are ever present when such large numbers of birds crowd into huge nesting colonies. Pallas's Fish Eagles *Haliaeetus leucoryphus* are resident birds of prey, and these are joined by several other species of eagle, including Spotted *Aquila clanga*, and Crested Serpent Eagle *Spilornis cheela*, but by far the most actively aggressive predator is the Marsh

A Great White Egret chick begs for food.

Harrier *Circus aeruginosus*. It is difficult to miss its swoop and its sometimes Peregrine-like dive. Its very presence causes chaos among the tightly packed feeding birds. Scavengers range from monitor lizards *Varanus monitor* to Adjutant and Lesser Adjutant Storks, as well as Black (Pariah) Kites *Milvus migrans* and vultures of several species.

Among the smaller waterbirds, the most striking and numerous are the Purple Gallinule *Porphyrio porphyrio* and the Coot *Fulica atra*, but several species of crake are present, as well as the spectacularly beautiful Pheasant-tailed *Hydrophasianus chirurgus* and Bronze-winged Jacanas *Metopidius indicus*. Lapwings, plovers and other waders, though never abundant, make

Bar-headed Geese arrive from beyond the Himalayas to winter here. Jet airline pilots have reported seeing them flying alongside them well above the highest peaks.

Young White Ibis gather together when they leave the nest, but they still beg for food from their parents for several weeks before they become completely independent.

Spotbill.

In flight Whistling Duck wheel and
turn uttering their high pitched calls
which give them their name.

A Bronze-winged Jacana picks its
way through the waterside vegetation.

up a bewildering variety seen in few other places. Swimming between the banks and the reed-beds, Garganey *Anas querquedula*, Cotton Teal *Nettapus coromandelianus*, Common *Aythya ferina* and Red-crested Pochards *Netta rufina*, Pintail *Anas acuta*, Mallard *A. platyrhynchos* and Common Teal *A. crecca* make up the bulk of the ducks. On the wet grasslands the Greylag *Anser anser* and Bar-headed Geese *A. indicus* stand sentinel over the Siberian White Cranes, while the noisy pairs of Sarus Cranes *Grus antigone* trumpet their fidelity or dance in unison, watched by a sambur buck *Cervus unicolor* or a party of blue bulls *Boselaphus tragocamelus*.

Of the other birds of the wetlands, five kingfishers are found here. The black and white Pied Kingfisher *Ceryle rudis* hovers and dives like a Kestrel *Falco tinnunculus*, and the small European species *Alcedo atthis* plunges from an overhanging branch.

To the south of the reserve the sandy scrubland has numerous dryland species, ranging from rollers to parakeets, hoopoes to woodpeckers. At the aptly named Python Point, there are deep holes where these large snakes *Python malurus* bask in the sun, disappearing underground with deceptive speed if one ventures close.

I have visited Bharatpur many times. All of India protects its birds, unlike other eastern lands where only priests or princes afford sanctuary. As in much of the world, however, the very pressures of population mean the crowding out of birds and animals to provide living space for people, and the need for havens like the Keoladeo National Park grows daily more urgent. It is fortunate that the present government of India sees the need to conserve its wildlife. Elsewhere in Asia, the human tide has advanced too quickly.

5 India

Gujarat

The varying and conflicting factors which enable herons and other water birds to prosper are nowhere better illustrated than in a study of their strange, comparatively recent, occupation of their habitat in the State of Gujarat in Western India.

Except in the towns and villages, much of the farmland of the regions of Gujarat, Shaurastra and Kutch is almost entirely devoid of trees, due mainly to years of continual drought, together with the ever-increasing need for fuel.

At one time mangrove forests stretched down almost the entire coastline, but as the need for cattle fodder, firewood and timber became more and more urgent, large cutting of the mangroves meant their virtual destruction in many areas. Indeed only on and around the islands in the Gulf of Kutch does any mangrove remain.

The loss of trees of any size has meant the local extinction of the large Black-necked Stork *Ephippiorhynchus asiaticus*, but other species of birds have moved to the town and villages where large trees still exist. So along the

Laden with mangrove cut from an island in the Gulf of Kutch these fishermen return to the mainland to sell their cargo to farmers. The former dense strands of mangrove found all round the coast and islands of Kutch and Shirastra have been cut down to sea level and thus can no longer protect the shrimp and small crustaceans on which the fish feed. So the fishermen are losing their livelihood as the formerly abundant fish stocks dwindle, and the farmers, having destroyed their own trees, now have to pay a heavy price for fodder and firewood. Only slowly is it being realised that by destroying the mangrove barriers erosion accelerates and all wildlife suffers.

Every large tree is crowded with
nests at the Reef Heron colony.

Even telegraph poles are used for nesting sites as the spaces for nests are cramped with birds.

Next page. Reef Herons, which used to nest on the mangrove swamps around the coast, now occupy all the trees in the port area of Bhavnagar ignoring the heavy movement of trains as ships are loaded and unloaded, Dockers in the port take pride in watching over these birds and the night watchmen on the port area guard the nesting trees throughout the long season.

A mixed morph pair – both in courtship colors. The sitting white bird shows aggression to a dark bird in courtship colors.

A pair of white-phased birds in courtship colors.

coastal towns, Asiatic *Threskiornis melanocephalus* and Black Ibis *Pseudibis papillosa* join Large White Egrets *Egretta alba*, as well as Little Egrets *Egretta garzetta* and the ubiquitous Cattle Egrets *Bubuleus ibis*, in the middle of quite large towns. The loss of the mangrove, the natural home of the Reef Heron, has caused this specialized feeder either to join the other birds in mixed colonies, or form colonies of its own, in well-protected areas of trees in temple grounds, factory sites and ports.

Many of these species feed on the abundant supply of mud skippers found on the muddy flats and tidal estuaries, but even where such food is available there are whole areas where no birds are to be found.

Apart from food the most important requirement is a safe place for these

Courtship displays involve stick pre-
sentation and here an immature grey
bird with a pale breast attempts to
pair-bond with a dark mature bird.

Four well-grown white-phased chicks find their stick nest only just big enough to hold them. Many birds fall to the ground at this stage of their development. The dark-coloured phased bird has still not lost its bright courtship plumes.

This dark-phased parent has lost most of its breeding plumes now that the chicks are well grown.

A dark-phased chick which has a typical Reef Heron bill.

birds to nest and this is provided in areas of the State of Gujarat by the deeply religious and cultural habits of most of the Hindu population. Quite apart from the many Jain peoples who will harm no living creature, there are many who are vegetarians and others, such as some farmers, who will protect birds and other creatures even if their behaviour spoils crops or does other damage.

The pattern is clear for any conservationist to see. Fishermen and people of different cultures along the coast, where there are often apparently suitable trees for nesting, will allow destruction of nesting birds, whereas in areas where life is sacred the birds remain unharmed.

This unique situation has allowed the Reef Heron to move onto the coastline, and here in suitable areas it nests in large numbers. Some birds begin as early as April, but others join the colony until as late as mid-August, forming a long continuous breeding period. Towards the middle of this long protracted nesting season the arrival of the ibises and other herons means competition for not only nest spaces, but also for scarce nesting material.

There is no similar set of circumstances anywhere in India or indeed to my knowledge anywhere in the world. Until the late Professor R M Naik and his students found these colonies of Reef Herons, it was quite clearly understood that this was a well-described bird with two well-marked dark and light morphs. Indeed there had been considerable doubt as to whether

This dark-phased bird has been feeding in the mud. Leg and feet colours are often obscured and with so many color variations great care has to be taken when recording them.

the two morphs interbred, except on rare occasions. Even so its general plumage and soft-part colours were well established.

When, following the publication of *The Herons of the World*, Dr Naik summoned me to come to Gujarat, I had expected to see these birds in well-recognized forms even though nesting in unfamiliar surroundings. My surprise was complete, however, when I arrived at a large colony at the new port of Bhavnagar. The nests were built in large trees overlooking the port, and the continuous activity of loading and unloading, loud shunting of trains and other vehicles was ignored, as these multicoloured birds courtship-displayed, laid their eggs and raised their variously plumaged young.

The numerous lessons to be learnt from this quite incredible colony, and from many others like it along the coast, have caused considerable reappraisal of Little Egret/Reef Heron taxonomic grouping as well as its use of plumage both in courtship behaviour and final pair-bonding.

Indeed there is only one unaltered trait throughout these breeding

A partly coloured dark-phased bird uses its head plumes in an aggressive display. The red lores indicate that it is in full courtship condition.

Multi-coloured chicks with a dark morphed parent behind and a pale morphed bird on the branch above.

Next page. A dark phased bird in full breeding plumage. Bill, lores and feet are all red.

colonies, and that is the flushing of the lores to red during courtship. Otherwise birds will mate even if one is an immature bird with no so-called 'aigrette plumes'. Spectacular plumed birds appear to use their 'aigrettes' not to attract mates but to repel would-be intruders. Such factors are crying out for detailed behavioural studies.

Dark, light or multi-coloured morphs interbreed, and the variation in soft part colour including bill and legs follows no recognizable pattern. Nestlings vary widely in colour, and whilst bill size seems to conform to that of the well-described stouter bill of the Reef Heron, some birds have thinner bills more akin to Little Egrets.

Dr Naik's careful papers recognizing this situation clearly reached the conclusion that interbreeding between Little Egrets and both colour morphs of the Reef Heron is taking place, and I have concurred with this. Apparent interbreeding on a much smaller scale has occurred in inland lakes in East

The thin black bill of this white-morphed bird contrasts with the yellow bill of similar plumed birds.

Africa and the recognition that this forms a single species with varying races has been widely accepted. The final acceptance of this somewhat radical concept however awaits detailed DNA analysis to receive full acceptance by a somewhat reluctant ornithological establishment.

It is clear that if these birds are given continued protection their adaptability will enable them to find ways to survive. This survival, however, may come at the cost of loss of genetic differentiation that took thousands of years to create.

This white morphed bird in courtship colors has a yellow bill.

Nowhere in Asia is the Black Ibis
found in such numbers as it is in
Gujarat. Every ditch and dike in
villages throughout the state have
one of these spectacular birds
feeding quite tamely. Elsewhere it
is a shy bird, but the benign culture
of the people of this state ensures
that it prospers.

One of the many islands in the bay
of Kutch. The bushes on them are
mainly cactus and many species nest
on them, now the mangrove has
gone.

6 **India**

Along the Brahmaputra River

In the East, it is customary to take exercise early in the day, and across the parade grounds of Northern India recruits to the rapidly expanding wartime army of the early 1940s stamped over the dusty maidans as dawn broke. Only at this time of the day is the air cool, as summer approaches. Relief comes with the start of the early monsoon rains. With the rains there came a strange ungainly spectator to these activities. It strutted with a slow martial gait as though inspecting the assembled troops. Well named the Adjutant Stork, it appeared every year at this time with unfailing regularity.

All over Northern India this huge stork was to be found singly or in small groups scavenging at refuse dumps, probing in the ponds and jeels, consuming with great gulps anything and everything that came its way. Then as the cooler weather arrived, it departed as mysteriously as it had arrived.

Nearly a century before, a colony of this bird had nested in the Sunderbands, but this had disappeared decades before the Second World War.

These local people do not harm the storks that nest in their villages, but often, when they want to expand their fields, they will chop down the nesting trees.

(a) A female Greater Adjutant Stork arrives and performs 'Balancing Posture'. The male is the top bird on the right. Both birds are silent at the start of this display.

(b) The female spreads her wings and begins to lower her head. The male crouches with his pouch extended.

(c) The female begins to lower her head, whilst the male begins to raise his head. The pouch is now retracted.

(d) The female's head is completely lowered. The male raises its head and fully extends his pouch. This is a version of the 'Up-down' display with the bill open slightly.

Many decades before this, there had been two colonies in Southern Burma, and it was thought that these annual visitors came from there, as they had done for generations. In those days, across the Pegu plains of Southern Burma, vast armies of this stork had assembled in groups stretching as far as the eye could see. They dispersed after a few days to the two colonies. One of these was in the extensively flooded woodlands at the foot of the Pegu Hills, and here they shared the trees amicably with equal numbers of Spot-billed Pelicans *Pelecanus philippensis*. The other they occupied with Lesser Adjutant Storks *Leptoptilus javanicus* in the tall trees growing from the cliffs of the steep range of limestone rock called the Needong Hills, which are about 25 miles up the Ataran river, south east of Moulmein towards the Thai border. During the peaceful years between the two World Wars Burma developed a prosperous rice-growing industry, and the whole of the flooded forest areas of Pegu were cleared to form one of the great 'rice bowls' of Asia. Albeit briefly, the fringes of this area contained some trees. The day of this huge assemblage of birds was over, and by the beginning of the Second World War no trace of them could be found. The Japanese invasion which swept through from Thailand finally put paid to any further nesting of this once abundant bird whose colonies had held the greatest concentration of storks in the world. Like the Open-billed Storks *Anastomus oscitans*, which still nests in Thailand, the Adjutant Storks had mainly dispersed westwards across the hills of Northern Assam, and followed the Brahmaputra river down the Nepalese Terai, and on to the northern plains of India. The fact that some continued to make this journey for almost 40 years after the war suggests that the birds had to be wanderers of great age. When good fortune led to the discovery of birds breeding

Sticks are carried in both bill and claws with huge wings and tail fully extended.

Previous page. Greater Adjutant Stork. Its strong bill enables it to crunch bones and   swallow all sorts of strange objects. It was thought until recently to be extinct as a nesting bird.

Birds gather in ponds and sewage dumps in the main cities along the river, and are greatly valued as scavengers. Why their relation the Marabou, in Africa, has prospered and they have not is puzzling.

in Assam, it quickly became apparent that these birds were non-migratory, and thus they were never visitors to India.

In 1967 Dr Philip Khal had photographed a pair at a single nest in the Kashiranga National Park, and as late as 1983 G L Ouwneel of Holland found a few nests again in the park, but none elsewhere in Assam. It began to look as though one more large and distinguished species was well on the road to extinction.

In February 1990 I was asked to give a paper on herons at the Seminar of Wetland Ecology in Bharatpur. As I awaited my turn to speak a young man began to talk on his work in Assam. His name was Prasant Saikia, and he was a student of Dr P C Bhattercharjee, a Professor at the University of Gauhati. I sat in amazement as his tale unfurled. It seems that on an expedition along the banks of the Brahmaputra river seeking data for his Master's Degree on the behaviour of the Lesser Adjutant Stork, he had found, near the village of Barpeta (some hundred kilometres away), a colony of not Lesser, but Greater Adjutant Storks. Their nests were high up in tall

With wings fully extended each primary is separated as this huge stork glides overhead.

The Lesser Adjutant Stork seen here on the water hyacinth growing along the river bank is a much commoner bird, and its range extends throughout the Oriental Region.

trees which were mostly screened by large stands of bamboo. Riding his bicycle (for this was his only means of transport) he had followed his discovery by finding more nests in other scattered villages along the river. A more detailed survey found no less than 75 pairs nesting in various villages during the winter of 1989.

I made immediate arrangements to go to Assam. Visitors were not welcome because of the numerous problems of security due to fighting by insurgents, but I was eventually able to obtain a visa and arrived for the start of the breeding season in November.

Dr Bhattercharjee and some of his students from the University took me to several of the small colonies along a stretch of the great river. The Brahmaputra winds across northern Assam, changing direction, sometimes annually, leaving mud banks and marshes on either side of its meandering course. Villages are situated on high ground and farmlands nearby are subject to flooding. The tall trees of the Simul *Bambax coibi* or Cotton Trees, Keda, *Anthrocephalus scolaris* and the 'Devil Tree' *Alstomia scolaris* contain as many as three nests each and are heavily screened by bamboo.

Farmland is at a premium, and the only way to extend the acreage under cultivation is to cut down trees. Thus the age-old problem rears its head yet again as the need to feed the ever-increasing population accelerates.

When the young birds fledge they disperse with the adult birds to sewage ponds and refuse dumps in the larger villages and towns. Their early need

Next page. Huge stick nests are renewed annually and are right at the top of trees. Often the foliage is destroyed by the acidic excreta and when this happens the birds will move to a different tree.

for a fish diet is replaced by an ability to consume whatever is edible. Indeed they have been recorded as swallowing almost anything from an old boot to a buffalo horn.

The dangers from such behaviour both at the nest and after post-breeding dispersal were obvious. Dr Bhattercharjee set up a wardening system. Farmers who wished to cut down trees were partially compensated, and villagers were asked to help in protecting the birds. Local people had previously been unaware of the rarity of these birds and by appealing to their pride, villagers reacted favourably. I talked with many village leaders and they expressed great interest. Support is now needed to provide transport for the University team and for compensating villages who agree not to chop down trees. It is hoped that this will eventually happen. I found, as so often in India, that local sympathy was present, but at more senior levels political will was lacking. The sterling work done by scientists and in universities deserves much more recognition from Central Government than it is currently receiving.

The enormous increase in confidence in India due largely to its huge economic expansion in recent years has unfortunately persuaded senior politicians that they do not need, and in some areas no longer welcome, assistance from outside bodies or individuals in the field of conservation. The driving force provided by the late Mrs Indhira Gandhi and for many years by Dr Salam Ali is sadly no longer apparent. Let us hope this will change.

7 China

The Zhalong Reserve, Heilanchiang Province

Harbin, the capital of the northeast province of Heilanchiang, is on the same latitude as the Canadian city of Montreal, and has a similar climate. To the northwest lies Quiquihar, a smaller town of some million people – for such populations are not considered large by Chinese standards – along the route of the trans-Siberian railway.

Both these towns are on the flat central plain of what was formerly called Manchuria. Besides the railway line, they are connected by the River Neinjiang, which rises in the mountains to the north. This river is fed by innumerable tributaries originating from the mountains of the Great Khingan Range to the west and the Lesser Khingan Range to the east. Some of the smaller rivers and streams from these ranges feed into lakes and ponds, rather than into the main river, and when the heavy winter snows melt they flood out over the plains.

One such river, the Wu-Yu, rises in the eastern ranges and feeds a huge area of permanent marsh with lakes, reed-beds and coarse grassy water meadows. This covers an area of 42,000 ha 30 km to the east of Quiquihar and has been established as the largest wetlands nature reserve in China, called the Zhalong Reserve.

Peasant communities around these swamps have traditionally harvested fish, reeds which are cut during the winter when they can be easily reached across the frozen waters, and eggs from the colonies of nesting birds.

During the Cultural Revolution from 1966 to 1971, the communes increased their robbing of nests, encouraged by Chairman Mao's 'three day war' declared on birds in 1958. This activity, aimed at rats, flies, 'sparrows' and other 'pests', was taken as a licence to kill all wildlife, and some reports claim that nearly one million birds were destroyed in that year, and many more thereafter. This period of devastation in China lasted until 1976, and teachers, scientists and other intellectuals were sent to work in the fields or imprisoned, leaving all universities and other places of learning largely unused.

Difficulty in penetrating the tangled vegetation and thick reed-beds during the summer months probably saved some of the large colonies of birds from being completely eradicated. Following the declaration of this area as a nature reserve, it is now the government's intention to develop a strategy

The Red Crowned Crane is revered as a symbol of long life and its statue is here in the grounds of the Forbidden City in Beijing.

Sequence of three pictures of the Red Crowned Crane dancing.

for conserving the wildlife of the region, and opening it up as an attraction for tourists. The main motivation for achieving this aim is the discovery of large numbers of breeding cranes of several species which have survived here. The Chinese revere the crane, which they consider a symbol of longevity, and paintings on parchment, canvas and pottery depict the Red-crowned Crane *Grus japonensis*, which has been adopted as the emblem of Heilanchiang Province.

Usually they dance together, but sometimes a single bird will excitedly perform on its own.

A Red Crowned Crane chick.
Hatched in this northern territory it
must quickly acquire flight feathers to
enable it to fly south before the ice
and snow cover this reserve,

For many decades this region of China has remained isolated from the
outside world and, since the eclipse of Russian influence here after the
Second World War, very few Westerners, and only an occasional Japanese
group, have been allowed permits to visit. Now that the decision to allow
tourists to come and see the wildlife of the area, and in some cases to hunt
in it, has been made, it is possible to join an organized tour of this region,
although facilities are still minimal and the cost high.

The journey to Zhalong is long and wearisome, and once there the enormity of the task of birdwatching quickly becomes evident. Very limited channels of clear waterways have been cut through the reeds, and rather fragile punts are used to travel into the fringes of the seemingly endless marsh. Some hours of punting bring some sign of birdlife, and on our first visit a very large colony of nesting Purple Herons *Ardea purpurea* was reached. At a rough estimate it held about 5000 nests and nearly all contained newly hatched young at this time in mid July. Further progress was impossible as the day was rapidly drawing on, and in any case by this stage the reeds were too tightly packed for us to advance any farther.

By peering over the tall vegetation it was possible to glimpse Oriental White Ibis *Threskiornis aethiopicus melanocephalus*, Grey Heron *Ardea cinerea* and European Spoonbill *Platalea leucorodia* circling some distance away, and it was evident that there was a considerable-sized mixed colony further on. What other species it contained was a matter of conjecture, and has yet to be established even by the Chinese scientists working here.

The sense of frustration at being so near and yet so far from an obvious wealth of bird species was to be a constant feature of this visit. Perhaps eventually trails will be cut and covered approaches built, both for scientific observation and possibly for tourists, but for the present there is neither the facility nor are there the people able to give any reliable information as to

A large colony of European Spoonbills make the long journey northwards across China to nest here. Although the Black-faced Spoonbill had been reported from near here, we were disappointed not to find it.

The Falcated Teal are rare visitors to
the reserve.

what species are present. The staff at Shalong rely mainly on collecting
specimens and eggs, for they have no field guide and no binoculars.
Knowledge was acquired in Victorian times in this manner, and it is how it
is done in China today. It is evident that the Chinese are some 40 years
behind in their ornithological expertise. Like the early Victorians in Britain,
the Chinese conservationists invariably capture samples of all rare species
for zoos and captive breeding. Here at Zhalong, both Red-crowned Cranes
and White-naped Cranes *Grus vipio* are taken from the nest and hand-
reared. It is stated also that a third species may nest here, namely the
Demoiselle Crane *Anthropoides virgo*.

It is quite likely that this reserve holds the largest breeding population of
the Red-crowned Crane left in the world, and some estimates have put the
numbers at up to 100 breeding pairs. Professor Ma Yiching of the Institute
of Natural Resources in Harbin, however, carried out ground and aerial surveys in the period between 1980 and 1982 and estimated the total population to be in the region of 500 individuals. In the Soviet Union, nothing like
this number now breed. Their main breeding grounds are just across the
border in the Soviet Far East, as it is called. In the Khanku Lake basin, the
Bola basin and the lower regions of the Bureya river and the middle Zeya
river, Red-crowned Cranes are reported by Dr Yuri Shibnev not to exceed
20 nesting pairs in any one area, and considerably fewer in most areas sur-

veyed. Japan is the only other region in which this species breeds, and here again captive breeding is extensively carried out. The White-naped Crane and the Common Crane *Grus grus* nest in Zhalong and their numbers are estimated to be 34 and 84 birds, respectively.

The International Crane Foundation, based in the USA and led by a Canadian, Dr George Archibald, considers this to be the most important area for cranes in the world. This is reinforced by the fact that, besides the three or four breeding species, two others migrate through here, and it is thus theoretically possible to see six species of crane in one day in this one place. The Foundation is working closely with both the Harbin authorities and the reserve staff; using the expertise of this organization, it is expected that much will be achieved to protect this unique sanctuary, with an established scientific programme of captive breeding and a monitoring programme for this key area.

This female Hen Harrier at the nest is one of no less than four species of Harrier we found in the Zhalong area. We found it difficult to differentiate the females in flight. The Hen Harrier may well have been the least common.

White-naped Cranes nest here, but are somewhat rarer than the Red Crowned.

The two species moving through are the rare Hooded Crane *Grus monacha* and the rarest of all species, the endangered Siberian White Crane *G. leucogeranus*. This latter species was seen here in April 1982, and 170 birds were counted on their way north from the wintering grounds of the marshes of the Yangtze. This probably represents the total eastern population of this species, the remainder wintering in India and Iran.

The migratory routes of most of the eastern wetland birds through this region can only be surmised. It is highly unlikely that there will ever again be any programme of ringing – called by Americans 'banding' – on the scale of the MAPS programme discussed elsewhere in this book. It is unfortunate that, for political reasons at that time, China's ornithologists did not participate in this great endeavour. Not only did they not ring birds, they did not report the many ringed birds that must have been found in China. Dr Cheng Hso-tsin, the doyen of China's few ornithologists, has agreed that the routes of migration across China are not well known; his previous reviews, however, suggest that birds from eastern China originating from the far northeast move either directly south, to follow the coastline into southern China and southeast Asia, or move into Korea and then southwards over the sea to Taiwan or in some cases eastwards to Japan. Whatever the truth of this is, it is certain that Zhalong lies in the path of a migration route between the eastern Siberian breeding grounds of large numbers of bird species,

including waders and waterfowl as well as Ciconiiformes and many passerine species, and the numerous wintering grounds from Japan's Pacific coast southwards to the Philippines and, in the case of wading birds, as far as the coasts of Australasia.

At this (eastern) end of the Palearctic region, which stretches from Iceland across Eurasia to Japan, waterfowl winter in large numbers in Japan, whereas cranes and storks enter southern China, where they stay for the winter unless forced further south by unseasonably bad weather. Certainly, the discovery of the wintering grounds of the Siberian White Cranes, on Lake Payang in the Kiangsi Province of central China, reinforces this; it is known, too, that five species winter on the lower reaches of the Yangtze river, and that flocks of Hooded Cranes also winter at Shengjin Lake in An-hwei Province. Undoubtedly, many heron, ibis and spoonbill species join birds from Japan, Korea and Taiwan to winter in the Philippines, but others travel overland to southern China and often onwards to Thailand and Malaya. The discovery of small numbers of the rare Swinhoe's Egret *Egretta eulophotes* wintering in Malaya confirms this.

Recently, too, we have learnt that the elusive Black-faced Spoonbill *Platalea minor* winters near Hanoi in Vietnam. It previously bred in small numbers in Korea, but is seldom seen there now. It has long been stated that its main breeding grounds were near Harbin in China, and this was the

Around the reserve in the drier woodland areas, the Siberian Rubythroat nests.

discovery I had hoped to make in Shalong. Whether or not it is there has not been proved, and its discovery would be a major triumph for China were it to be found. As absolutely nothing is known of its ecology, and as it is considered to be an endangered species, one hopes that it will not join the ranks of extinct species without any knowledge having been obtained of its requirements for successful breeding.

Waders and terns travel much longer distances on migration, and many pass through Shalong. Undoubtedly, these arrive in Australia, some perhaps stopping en route. We found White-winged Black Terns *Chlidonias leucopterus* in a loose colony in the grasslands inundated by water in the reserve, their heavily blotched eggs as yet unhatched in July; I saw birds of this species in the following spring on the sewage ponds of Darwin in Australia. It is intriguing to consider the possibility that I saw the same birds at both ends of their considerable range.

In these same Zhalong wetlands, thick, tall vegetation grew to heights of 7-8 feet (2-2.4 m), and while walking through these waterlogged fields the boom of the Eurasian Bittern *Botauras stellaris* was heard from all sides. This species, now rather rare in western Europe, was present here in considerable numbers. Making short, feeble flights ahead of us, two of the smaller bitterns gave us short looks at them: the Chinese Yellow Bittern *Ixobrychus sinensis*, aptly named by the Russians the 'Long-nosed Bittern' was common; but also present was the smaller Schrenck's Bittern *I. eurhythmus*, very similar in colour pattern to the European Little Bittern *I. minutus*.

Dr Christopher Perrins of the Edward Grey Institute at Oxford, who accompanied me on this visit, saw a number of species of waders the following year on his return visit. These included Common Sandpipers *Actitis hypoleucos*, Marsh Sandpipers *Tringa stagnatilis*, Spotted Redshanks *T. erythropus* and Greenshanks *T. nebularia*, Curlew Sandpipers *Calidris ferruginea* and Long-toed Stints *C. subminuta* and others, among them the Avocet *Recurvirostra avosetta*. None of these birds, however, appeared to be breeding and they were probably early passage migrants.

A strong feature of this complex wetland ecosystem is the mixture we found of birds still breeding in July together with others which had either completed their cycle locally somewhat earlier, or were moving through from a more northerly breeding area.

Of the passerines, warblers were actively calling in the reeds. Although they were difficult to observe, we identified Black-browed *Acrocephalus bistrigiceps* and Great Reed Warblers *A. arundinaceus*. Both Japanese *Emberiza yessoensis* and European Reed Buntings *E. schoeniclus* on the other hand were more easily seen, and seemed likely still to be nesting. In the woodland areas Siberian Rubythroats *Luscinia calliope* had young in the nest, whereas titmice, nuthatches *Sitta* sp., and white-eyes *Zosterops* sp., had already formed post-breeding foraging parties. A similar situation applied to swallows: European Swallows *Hirundo rustica* were already perched in parties on the overhead wires, while Red-rumped Swallows *H. daurica* were busy building their bottle-shaped nests on the walls of the reserve buildings.

The stretches of open water held Moorhens *Gallinula chloropus*, Coots *Fulica atra* and a few ducks, notably Baer's Pochard *Aythya baeri*. Herring Gulls *Larus argentatus* were seen singly, and Black Tern *Chlidonias niger*, Whiskered Tern *C. hybridus*, Little (Least) Terns *Sterna albifrons* and Common Terns *S. hirundo* were all identified.

The dryer ground certainly had Great Bustards *Otis tarda*, and we were shown an egg of this species. Lapwings *Vanellus vanellus* flew constantly overhead, as did the Pied Harrier *Circus melanoleucus*. The handsome male bird was very prominent and easily identified, but the browner female is very like the female Hen Harrier *C. cyaneus*, and indeed like the female Pallid Harrier *C. macrourus*. All three species may well have been present in the area.

Further away from the marsh there is a traditional nesting site of the Oriental White Stork *Ciconia (ciconia) boyciana*, not recognized in China as a separate species from the western one but

Chinese boatmen punt along narrow canals cut through the thick reed beds. They take eggs from the nests they find. This is the only way of finding out what species are here!.

thought by many to be so, and distinguished by its black rather than red bill.

The checklist of birds of this area is based on the official Chinese Preliminary List (1983), but includes all the additional species identified on visits made by myself, Dr Perrins, and Dr MacDonald in 1981; Dr Perrins and his group in 1982; and Mr Jeffery Boswall and his party in 1983. It is by no means complete. Dr Cheng's handbook, although not yet translated from the Chinese, has detailed maps of most species, but Dr Cheng himself would be the first to admit that this does not give a modern picture of the situation, which must await a more detailed study than has been done in recent years.

Undoubtedly, this important Chinese wetland contains some fascinating species, perhaps some as yet unrecorded.

8 Japan

The Shinhama Reserve, Chiba, Tokyo

Until a very few years ago the estuary of the River Edo was a vast area of marshland and tidal flats. This area, east of the Japanese capital, lies at the head of Tokyo Bay in the Prefecture of Chiba.

Ducks and wading birds arrive here in huge numbers from their breeding grounds to winter in this temperate Pacific coastal region of Japan, which is the main wintering area for most of the ducks which breed in the Eastern Palearctic. It is also an important staging post for many species of wading birds on migration to and from the Australasian coasts.

Duck preserves were established at many places in Japan and reached

Scaup in the Shinhama reserve.

Above left. Turnstones. These birds travel huge distances using Japan as a stopping off place. Many will go southwards as far as Australia.

Above right. Polluted grey skies at this heronry give warning of a sharp fall in breeding numbers. The growth in chemical manufacturing has raised the level of pollution around Tokyo.

their peak during the great Tokugawa period about 100 years ago, when some were built on the estates of the feudal lords. It may well be that many of the preserves are much older than this, but the idea was perhaps introduced by the Dutch, who traded here extensively from the early 17th century.

Three such preserves are administered by the Imperial Household of the Japanese Emperor, and the Shinhama Reserve in Chiba Prefecture is one of these. Permission to visit here was obtained for me initially some 20 years ago by Mr Dudley Cheke, who at that time was the Minister at the British Embassy. The uniqueness of the famous reserve lay in its closeness to Tokyo, in its use since the early 1920s as a bird-ringing station, and in the protection it gave to large numbers of breeding herons which built nests in the bamboo and pine trees surrounding the artificial duck ponds.

The ponds are linked to a series of decoy canals along which the ducks are lured both by tame decoy ducks and by the prospect of food. At the Imperial reserves, the decoys are trained to come into the canals when they hear two pieces of wood being struck together. Elsewhere, food boxes are tapped and bait is supplied from bamboo pipes protruding from the hides towards the water, but a feature unique to the Imperial reserve is the use of bellows similar to those used by blacksmiths. When ducks stop at the entrance to a canal, the bellows unit is pressed, sending up air in a series of bubbles which frighten the ducks into the nets. There are a number of

methods of trapping the ducks once in the canals and ponds, but the Japanese use of hand-nets known as Sadi-ami is another singular feature, and this is still practised today.

Like all Japanese customs, the art of duck-netting was not only a practical form of capturing ducks for the pot, or providing sport for falconers, but also served as a ceremonial gathering for official and foreign diplomats. In former times, the Shogun and the Daimyo lords held political assemblies at duck-netting functions and took the opportunity to inspect the populations of such regions. In the early 1960s, when I was privileged to make my first visit to the heronry and duck preserve at Shinhama, it was still customary for these annual ceremonials to take place.

Mrs Dudley Cheke has kindly allowed me to quote from her splendid and evocative description of one of these historic visits, which served to bring the Imperial family of the Japanese Emperor closer to the outside world into which, until most recently, they seldom ventured.

'In the depths of winter, senior members of the Diplomatic Missions in Tokyo and their wives would be invited to Duck-Netting Parties at one of the Imperial Reserves.

'I never remember these occasions in dull weather or rain. It was windless, brilliant sunshine, blue sky and sharply cold: characteristic for the country in Japan during January and February.

The beautifully coloured male Mandarin Duck still breeds in its native land.

European Snipe are common visitors here.

'We had to get up early to arrive before 10 am; the warmest clothes were most necessary as there was a lot of standing about and chatting before the netting began. There were always members of the Imperial Family there as our hosts. They stood in a central position on the lawns and one particular Imperial Prince, who was a keen birdwatcher, would have a large bird-book opened at pictures of duck and he would point out which kinds we were likely to see and catch. The guests were mainly Diplomats, Service Attachés and members of the Ministry of Foreign Affairs. We surveyed each other with interest, not knowing which other countries would be represented that day nor what extraordinary clothes everyone would be wearing to keep warm.

'After a hot drink, we were divided into groups of ten, given careful instructions on how to conduct ourselves, handed a colossal "fishing"-type net on a long handle and led by a keeper to the entrance of a decoy channel. Half the group would take up station behind a bank on one side of the channel and half on the other side. On the very point of going to our positions we were firmly cautioned to maintain *complete silence* in order not to alert the duck. We went forward, bent double, keeping the nets low behind the bank, filled with tense anticipation and ambition. Once in position we waited, still bent double, for a given signal – this was disastrously difficult, because on catching a friend's eye we became hopelessly giggly – the strain and tension were tremendous.

'Of course we were all going to catch a duck – hadn't some of us played lacrosse? Suddenly the signal was given, we sprang up to peer over the bank – quacking ducks rising up and rushing at you – missed that one – here's another – missed that – someone has caught the Military Attaché from a friendly country and his head is all muddled up in the net ... Not so many people caught duck. Perhaps more practice was needed; but one was astounded – after all, the net was so *huge*. I never managed it on any occasion. If a duck was caught a keeper would spring to help extract it at once and we would all troop back to the main lawn where some of the ladies were given all the duck caught to release into the air, squawking back into freedom. These wild duck came to very little harm. A keeper stood nearby with a hooded falcon firmly attached to his arm.

'There was then much animated exchange of experiences which continued until we were ushered into a long, low building which housed wooden tables and benches. On these tables were tiny charcoal-burning stoves and small pieces of raw duck and vegetables piled in dishes. We took chopsticks and cooked our own food on the little stoves and the whole room became beautifully warm from the cooking, which was lovely as we had all been so cold. Warm *saké* also helped.

'Everyone was thawed out and happy and very international. I wrote to my mother: "I was sitting at a table with the Prince, the Russian Ambassador, the Australian Ambassadress and several people from the Japanese Foreign Office."

'As we were leaving, each family was presented with a brace of duck to take home – a truly delightful occasion.'

Duck-Netting at Imperial Reserves in Japan
(SHINHAMA and SAITAMA in the 1960s)
by Mrs Dudley Cheke

European Spoonbill.

Much more is known about the birds of the Shinhama Reserve than any other area of the east, as a ringing programme was carried out from as far back as 1924 right up until the start of the Second World War. This was re-activated under the MAPS programme between 1964 and 1970. While the main movements of ducks between the northern breeding grounds in Siberia and the Japanese coast were fairly predictable, it was surprising to find that in some years Pintails *Ianas acuta* from America's west coast find their way here. Equally surprising was the discovery that Ruddy Turnstones *Arenaria interpres* (the same pair being seen together here year after year) use this area as a stopping-off place for movement not only through Korea to Siberia, but also regularly northeastwards to the Pribilof Islands – from there flying southwards to the South Pacific and Australasia. This apparently separate population faces enormous hazards of weather and distance and many must perish.

The movement of herons along the far eastern migratory routes is now better known than that in the Western Palearctic. A detailed picture has emerged, which involved the ringing of thousands of Night Herons *Nycticorax mycticorax*, Little Egrets *Egretta garzetta*, Intermediate Egrets *E. intermedia*, Great White Egrets *E. alba* and the eastern race of the Cattle Egret *Bubulcus ibis coromandus*, all of which nest in the duck preserve.

Nearly all the breeding herons of Japan have been found to winter in the Philippines, though reaching these islands by different routes. Night

Previous page.
Above. A Grey Plover searches for food among the shells.
Below. A male Pochard.

Once much more common, the Intermediate Egret is a rare breeder in Japan today.

Herons and Cattle Egrets travel through Taiwan to join birds from the colonies breeding there, while Intermediate and Great White Egrets take a more southerly, direct route to Luzon and onwards into the central and southern archipelago. The exception to this migratory movement is the Little Egret, some 90% of which winter along the southern coastline of Japan, many travelling only a very short distance from their original breeding colony.

When I visited the colony in April, it was a stunning sight to see such large numbers of jostling egrets and herons nesting in a very limited area of bushes and trees. Bright courtship plumes were highlighted by the brilliant coloration of the lores, which at that time I was quite unprepared for. These colours are now well illustrated in the Japanese field guide.

The three all-white egrets were quickly identifiable by the colour of their so-called 'soft parts' – lores, bills, legs and feet. The Great White with its deep green lores stretching back behind the eye is the smaller eastern race *modesta*, and as such leaves no room for doubt as to its generic placing when seen in such conditions. The nominate race of the Intermediate Egret with its black bill and all black legs can easily be distinguished from the Little Egret here, for the latter has yellow feet which turn briefly to reddish-pink during courtship. Only far southwards in Indonesia, where the black-footed race of the Little Egret *migripes* occurs, do other identification features have to be considered.

On the duck ponds there were still large numbers. I saw Shoveler *Anas clypeata*, Pochard *Aythya ferina*, Common Teal *Anas crecca* and Baikal Teal *A. formosa*, Wigeon *A. penelope*, Tufted Duck *Aythya fuligula* and Pintail, as well as the more exotic Spotbill Duck *Anas poecilorhyncha* and Mandarin Duck *Aix galericulata*.

Many species breed in the area and others visit or pass through this refuge. Twenty years ago birds of prey were still seen in larger numbers than today, but it is interesting to see records of the trapping of such birds for falconry, which has been practised in Japan for centuries and which was still done up until recent times. The main area for the capture of birds of prey in later periods was the Okunoya beach near Kashima; plovers were used as decoys and the birds were trapped with bird-lime by a few traditional experts in the art.

Much has changed in Japan, as elsewhere, and the great modern industrial expansion into which these energetic people launched themselves affected both man and bird.

My visits in the 1960s were made at the start of an unprecedented period of expansion, and it was over ten years later before the opportunities came for me to revisit this famous sanctuary. By that time, the runaway industrial might of Japan had brought success around the world and disastrous pollution at home. The grey smog which surrounded Tokyo spread out to encompass the whole of Chiba Prefecture, and expansion for housing and factories meant the reclamation of swamplands, the filling-in of lotus-ponds and reed-beds and the industrial zoning of former rice-fields.

The numbers of herons breeding were down disastrously, and ducks were far less numerous than in the 1960s. Species of birds, which had totalled over 250 of the 480 found in Japan, were drastically reduced.

I returned depressed and deeply concerned. It seemed inevitable that the situation would continue, until in a few short years birds and their habitats would be completely eradicated from one of the East's greatest refuges. My concerns, however, were shared by others and the bird clubs and conservationists, of which there are many in Japan, have rallied at what must have been the eleventh hour.

In 1976 the Gyotoku Bird Observatory was opened and a further Wildlife Protective Area established, using two water barriers to reflood the land over some 54 ha; this, together with the Imperial Duck Refuge of 29 ha, created the new Shinhama Bird Reserve. New reed-beds have grown up; modern

Little Ringed Plover is a common summer visitor.

ecosystem-management techniques have resulted in the re-establishment of habitat suitable for feeding birds, both winter migrants and summer residents; and, while numbers, particularly of herons, are few compared with the period before industrial expansion, there is hope for a permanent reserve, managed to provide continuous refuge.

The popular upsurge of interest in conserving wildlife is gaining ground in Japan, and it is to be hoped that the threatened eradication of wetland habitats has been finally averted.

9 Indonesia

Pulau Dua

All central Java is mountainous, but as one travels westwards from the Indonesian capital, Jakarta, the land becomes flat and fertile and the paddy-fields stretch out across the plain. At the northwest tip of the island lies the small port of Karang Hantu, near the town of Bantam. This port was called 'The Gateway to Java' by the early Dutch and Portuguese traders coming from Sumatra. Until a few years ago a narrow shallow channel of water separated the sandy shore from the island of Pulau Dua – meaning literally 'island no. 2' – but silt has gradually closed the channel, and it is thus no longer an island. Covered in low bushes, the high ground to the north has a

Fishing boats along the coast. The shallow waters between Java and Sumatra are teeming with fish.

A Cattle Egret at its nest in full courtship colours. It is a much more highly coloured bird than its western relative,

few tall trees. Many of the bushes are overgrown with a species of *Convolvulus*, and in spring this small area of only an acre or so (0.4 ha) in size is the nesting area for over 5000 pairs of birds.

In so small a space, the distance between individual nests is very slight, and the opportunity to watch the interplay between individuals of several species is unrivalled anywhere. During the writing of *The Herons of the World* this remarkable heronry was my study area for the herons of southeast Asia, not only for observing behaviour, made easier by the height of the bushes which were no more than 10 feet (3 m) from the ground, but also because the various subspecies of white egrets here created a considerable challenge in identification.

The eastern race of the Great White Egret *Egretta alba modesta*, the smallest of the races of this worldwide species, is found from India eastwards into Australia, and I have become familiar with it throughout all those regions. It is for this reason that I have felt that the taxonomists who have sought to include it in the genus *Ardea* are incorrect. The behaviour, at least of this race, differs markedly from that of the true herons, and its close association with other egrets in this region strongly confirms my view that any such change of classification is hard to justify.

Certainly, the 'aerial display' spectacularly performed in full courtship attire can be seen here, and I have photographed it in a series of colour slides reproduced in this book. As this spectacular and unmistakable aerial flight is unrecorded in any of the large herons, this, together with other egret-like behaviour patterns, is a further reason to convince me that classification changes should be most carefully considered before such a radical alteration is made.

For a further challenge in identification, we need go no further than the next white egret species, the Intermediate Egret *E. intermedias*, as we some-what apologetically called it, for want of a more descriptive name, in *The Herons of the World*. This race is the nominate one, but going further east to Australia we find a different subspecies, *plumifera*, with a distinctive change in colour of the upper tarsus. While differences in size between this species and the larger Great White Egret are apparent when they are side by side, the totally black legs of both when breeding, though not when in courtship plumage, means that the coloration of the lores, or facial skin, is the most reliable feature difference; close examination is therefore required to be sure of identification.

The most reliable field mark is the noticeable extension of the lores to

This race of Little Egret has black feet but retains the blue-grey lores of the nominate race.

The Great White Egret has dark green lores and pink legs and feet during the breeding season.

well back behind the eye in the Great White Egret, but not in any other of the egret species. In the short period of full courtship plumage, as shown in the aerial display, the Great White Egret's normally black legs (but not always its feet) turn bright red or pink, and the facial skin an iridescent green. The difficulty again arises, however, when some individuals of this species have neither black legs, nor black bills, nor bright lores, and it is clear that these birds, although acquiring courtship plumes, are not fully mature. What their breeding success rate is it is hard to tell, but work carried out in other parts of the world on several species of heron suggests that it is not

usually very good. I have seen both brown-plumed immature Night Herons *Nycticorax nycticorax* and immature reddish-brown-capped Boat-billed Herons *Cochlearius cochlearius* in South America at nests containing eggs, but what their eventual success was I am unable to report. Efficiency in breeding is acquired by practice, and this is the case throughout the avian world.

The Little Egret *Egretta garzetta* here adds further to the problems of identification, as it is the subspecies *nigripes*, i.e. black-footed. Though a very occasional individual has yellow soles to its feet, it is in the Australian race

The Black-Crowned Night Heron is a great stealer of eggs and chicks from unattended nests in the heronry.

The spectacular 'Aerial Stretch' display of the eastern Great White Egret. This display has never been recorded before, and poses taxonomic questions as to its relationship with other races of this world-wide species.

Eastern Great White Egrets in conflict and at rest in the colony.

This Javanese Pond Heron is in full breeding plumage.

immaculata that the majority of birds have this variation. Should the Little Egret lose its diagnostic head plumes, which it quite often does here, as elsewhere, identification becomes even more difficult. Again, while the lores of this species are more noticeably pale in all races in the east, confusion occurs when, in courtship blush, red lores occur in most individuals; when this fades, there is no colour at all for a short period before the original is reasserted.

I have never succeeded in finding out whether in this challenging environment there are Eastern Reef Herons *Egretta sacra* of the white phase, but there are certainly some pairs of dark-phased birds. These differ markedly from the same species in Australia, being lighter grey and having pronounced white neck patches.

The eastern race of the Cattle Egret *Bubulcus ibis coromandus* nests in very large numbers and is the most numerous species in the colony. It is this race which spread in the last few decades to many parts of Australia.

Pulau Dua was an important ringing station during the MAPS programme, and under the leadership of Dr Somadikarta a team of three

workers ringed some 31 676 birds of 35 species on this island. This mammoth task was carried out over ten years, and clearly showed that, unlike northern egrets, these colonial nesters move only very short distances away from their breeding area in winter. While this is confirmed by ringing results from other stations, which show that the Philippines is the main wintering ground for northern migrants, there remains the possibility that the movement of southeastern Australian Cattle Egrets into New Guinea is paralleled by a movement from western and northern Australia through Indonesia. As there has never been a ringing programme in Australia's Northern Territory, and there is little likelihood of there being one for many years to come, this theory must remain as pure speculation.

One firmly sedentary species, however, is the Javanese Pond Heron *Ardeola speciosa*, and this beautifully plumed species has some 400 to 500 nesting pairs in Pulau Dua. Similarly, the Black-crowned Night Heron does not migrate south or east from here, though it has its usual post-breeding dispersal into eastern Java. The intriguing factor here is that a few pairs of the Australian species *Nycticorax caledonicus*, whose rufous coloration is indicated by its name Nankeen, do find their way to Java; the race concerned, *hilli*, appears, however, to be retracting its range, which at one time stretched as far as Japan, and is still reported from the Philippines. It has not been sighted on Pulau Dua to my knowledge since the 1960s.

Apart from egrets and small herons, both the Grey Heron *Ardea cinerea* and the Purple Heron *A. purpurea* are found here; neither has been proved to have moved any distance from these breeding grounds, and they are not

The tightly packed colony holds nesting birds of many species.

recorded from Australia. The race of the Grey Heron here, *rectirostris*, which is a much paler bird than the Western Palearctic race, was actually described by Gould in 1843 from a specimen reputedly found in New South Wales. This is, however, almost certainly an error brought about by incorrect labelling, which was so unfortunately prevalent in those early days of collecting, and which has led to much confusion and argument ever since.

The Purple Heron usually nests in reeds, but here is a tree-nester. The race is *manilensis*. Numbers on this island are dropping continually and it appears that this shy bird, like some of the stork species, is moving to the less disturbed island of Pulau Rambat and the other mixed breeding colony of birds off the coast nearer to Jakarta.

A similar movement between these two colonies occurs with the Oriental White Ibis *Threskiornis aethiopicus melanocephalus* and the Glossy Ibis *Plegadis falcinellus*. Both nest here intermittently in small numbers, but they are will o' the wisp and here, as elsewhere in the world, can be described as 'of no fixed abode'.

Unlike herons, which have survived remarkably well in the East, albeit in smaller numbers, many stork species are giving grave cause for concern. Here in Indonesia, the Milky Stork *Mycteria cinerea* nested on Pulau Dua when I first came in the 1970s; four pairs were successful. They have transferred their activities to Pulau Rambat, where they are holding their own. Outside Indonesia, this rare bird is known only from one colony of some 10-15 birds in Malaysia. Similarly, cranes in this part of Asia have suffered severely: records of Eastern Sarus Cranes *Grus antigone sharpii* show that its earlier range, in Burma and Thailand and southwards, has retracted to a few relict populations in the Philippines, Australia and possibly Vietnam of which today we have little or no reliable information.

Oriental Darters *Anhinga melanogaster* come to the island but do not nest here for some reason, perhaps because it is so crowded. A few Little Black Cormorants *Phalacrocorax sulcirostris* do nest, but are outnumbered ten to one by the Javanese Pygmy Cormorant *P. niger*, for which this is a major breeding ground. The rarer of the two, the Little Black Cormorant, is not mentioned in *A Field Guide to the Birds of South East Asia* (1975). It is found around most of the coastline and also in many places inland in Australia, and its toehold here in western Java is probably the limit of its range westward. It differs from the Javanese Pygmy Cormorant in having a distinct line of white nuptial plumes over the eye. The commoner cormorant is thought to be conspecific with the Pygmy Cormorant *P. pygmaeus* of the Western Palearctic.

There are, of course, numbers of smaller birds nesting within this bustling colony, and there is some predation from visiting birds of prey as well as scavenging by Brahminy Kites *Haliastur indus*. On the ground, the large monitor lizard *Varanus salvator* also scavenges. This fearsome-looking creature foraged for food scraps under my string bed one night while I was sleeping on the island, and I awoke with something of a start as it snapped its not inconsiderably sized jaws. This reptile keeps the undergrowth free of the carcases of dead chicks, which inevitably fall or are pushed from the crowded nests above in the struggle for survival.

The most feared bird to soar overhead, causing considerable disturbance, is the White-bellied Sea Eagle *Haliaeetus leucogaster*, but like others of its genus around the world it probably takes more young than fully adult herons or other nesting birds.

Brahminy kite scavenges around the heronry.

Apart from natural predation, such islands as this have been subjected in the past to the ravages of plume-hunters, who sailed from the South China Seas to shoot all the adult white breeding herons they could find, leaving the young helpless in their nests. In most years recently, the threat has been from fishermen who rob the nests of eggs. These fishermen construct bamboo platforms out in the shallow waters of the sea between Java and Sumatra, and travel in small, single-sail ketches or dug-out canoes.

Pulau Dua and other breeding islands have been protected by law for a number of years now, but at the end of the MAPS ringing programme there was no warden in Pulau Dua for the early part of one season and all the first clutches of eggs were stolen. It is interesting to note that all the species present resumed laying immediately, with the sole exception of the Intermediate Egret, which left the island until the following year.

This example of behaviour is but one instance that I can quote to suggest that the Intermediate is the least adaptable of the white egrets, and the one therefore at greatest risk. Fluctuations in the fortunes of all the colonial-nesting birds are bound to occur, but some species are certainly much more adaptable than others.

This island, under enlightened conservation, provides safe breeding ground. This requirement together with ample food resources, found presently in the paddyfields and along the shoreline, are the two factors necessary for the survival of the dwindling breeding stocks of these wetland birds.

Offshore, well-wardened sites such as this provide havens for a wide variety of wading birds, as human population expansion makes the mainlands of such rapidly developing countries untenable. The new danger which is present here, as in so many areas in the East, is the discovery of offshore oil. Pollution from oil spillage could quickly herald the extinction of the struggling avifauna, which is already in retreat from the advancing tide of human expansion at a rate never before known in history.

While ever hopeful, it seems extremely doubtful if such sights as are witnessed on the densely packed, vigorously alive Pulau Dua heronry can expect to be in existence in a generation or two from now.

10 **Australia**

Darwin and the South Alligator River

Beginning in November, the northeast Asia monsoon gathers force across the warm seas of the Indonesian archipelago, bringing a continuous hot, wet season which lasts until March and with each day brings rain, and each month a tropical cyclone. Even by April, when the wind changes and the Southeast Trade Winds blow, they first bring the 'knock 'em down' storms of Aboriginal folklore. Thereafter the warm, dry air blows throughout the Australian winter months. This is the climate at the Top End of the Northern Territory.

The rivers flow from the rocky sandstone ridges and meander through areas of swamp, mangroves, and grassy tidal flats as they approach the sea. There are *Pandanus* and Cabbage-tree palms *Roystoneo*, mangrove bushes, and forests of eucalyptus, paper barks *Melaleuca leucadendron* and cypress pine *Callitris*, and among them the tall termite mounds which stand like huge brown statues.

Fogg dam is famous for its birds and its water lilies.

The Australian Sacred Ibis is a distinct race of this wide spread species.

During the 'wet', the abundant fresh water mixes with the sea water across the tidal flats. The rivers rise and fall up to an incredible 20 feet (6 m) as they approach the sea. The open wet grasslands become rich in nutrients, and insect life, crustaceans, fish and plant life flourish and sustain huge populations of breeding and migrating birds, as well as mammals and reptiles. There are species of birds here which are found nowhere else, and even those species which are cosmopolitan in distribution have developed characteristics which enable them to be quickly recognized as unique races.

Along the coastline and on the muddy river banks, hundreds of thousands of wintering waders and terns change in March into their summer plumes. They are fattened by the abundant food supply, and thus are well prepared to make their long flights northwards to their breeding grounds on the tundra of Siberia and the endless stretches of dense reed-beds and grasslands of northwest China, joining the booming European Bitterns and the flocks of cranes.

Lively little Terek Sandpipers *Xenus cinereus* with upturned bills feed

This young Black-necked Stork is a common sight across the flood plains. Adult birds have red legs.

at measured intervals along the coast, turning the pale mudflats into polkadot patterns for as far as the eye can see. Godwits, Greenshanks *Tringa nebularia*, Far Eastern Curlews *Numenius madagascariensis*, Whimbrels *N. phaeopus*, Lesser Golden Plovers *Pluvialis dominica*, Lesser (Mongolian) Sand Plovers *Charadrius mongolus*, Ruddy Turnstones *Arenaria interpres* and Grey-tailed Tattlers *Heteroscelus brevipes* crowd along the banks at high tide.

The largest of terns, the Caspian *Sterna caspia* with dark red bill, contrasts with the smallest, the yellow-billed Little Tern *S. albifrons*, and over the billabongs sweep flocks of White-winged Black Terns *Chlidonias leucopterus*. Herons, egrets, kingfishers, ducks, bustards, kites, parrots, pigeons, honeyeaters and flycatchers form part of the 280 species of bird. Bats predominate in a total of 52 species of mammal. There are over 100 reptiles, with the dangerous saltwater crocodile *Crocodylus porosus* and at least five poisonous snakes to deter the unwary visitor.

Magic it may be, but idyllic it is not! To see these wonders is difficult and

Grey-tailed Tattlers travel long distances to nest in northern Europe.

often dangerous. Apart from the unpredictable sharp-toothed crocodiles, and the snakes, along the seashore is the venomous box-jellyfish *Chiropsalmus*, called locally the sea-wasp, whose tentacles give an often fatal sting.

The fast-running tides and submerged mudflats make the rivers a nightmare to navigate; bush fires sweep through the dry woodland as the water retreats and, to add to all this, large herds of water buffalo *Bubalus bubalis* introduced from southeast Asia, where they are docile creatures, have become as wild and treacherous as their African relatives. To witness the scene makes the hazards seem worthwhile. Nowhere else in the world can the naturalist see 100 000 Magpie Geese *Anseranas semipalmata* surveying the scene on upraised legs. Nowhere else does the compact little yellow-legged Pied Heron *Egretta picata* nest, or the rare Yellow Chat *Ephthianura crocea* appear, flitting through the reeds.

As the season turns from wet to dry, the change is marked by the arrival of flocks of southern-nesting Straw-necked Ibises *Threskiornis spinicollis*, Yellow-billed Spoonbills *Platalea flavipes* and the Red-tailed Black Cockatoo *Calyptorhynchus magnificus* called 'the heralds of the dry'.

When to visit this little-known region of Australia is a matter of choice. Movement is difficult during the rains, and indeed for some time thereafter, but too long a delay means that the active colonies of nesting herons, ibises and spoonbills, and the cormorants, Darters *Anhinga melanogaster* and other attendant species will have completed the year's breeding cycle. Detailed information from first-hand reports on the few active colonies on the Alligator rivers is hard to obtain, but what emerges is that the cycle of breeding begins in November. The early heron species are Cattle Egrets *Bubulcus ibis coromandus* and Nankeen Night Herons *Nycticorax caledonicus*, and almost certainly Great White Egrets *Egretta alba modesta*. We saw flights of immature Nankeen Night Herons and Cattle Egrets, reinforcing

The Salt-water Crocodile comes up into fresh water to breed. It waits under the heronry for the young birds that often fall into the water. This is the most fearsome of all crocodiles and is one of the reasons why the Australian Outback is no place for the careless.

Feral Buffalo came to Australia from India to pull the early settlers' wagons. No longer needed, they run wild and are extremely dangerous. Watching birds in Northern Australia is not for the faint hearted!

these reports on timing of nesting, but there is no official annual survey.

The South Alligator river colony had an interesting combination of nesting species at different stages of breeding. The Plumed or Intermediate Egret *E. intermedia plumifera* was the predominant species; most of its young were downy nestlings, but some were a few weeks older while a few were fully fledged. A small number of Great White Egrets had older chicks. Some Little Egrets *E. garzetta immaculata* were seen, though they were in full breeding plumage.

The most interesting species, which has hardly ever been observed and

Yellow-billed Spoonbills rarely travel to the Northern Territories.

seldom reported upon, was the Pied Heron. About a third of the herons present were of this species and, of these, half were sitting on eggs. Immature birds were present in a variety of plumages. Fully fledged young have white heads and were thought by early observers, including Sharpe in 1898 and Matthews in 1915, to be a different species. Some birds had brown head plumes, this presumably being a stage between nestling down and immaturity. It seems likely, though it is unproven, that the white-headed immatures moult in the spring following hatching, but it may well be that this plumage is retained for 12 months or more in similar manner to that of the Little Blue Herons *E. caerulea* of the New World. Certainly, away from the colony at the sewage farms in Darwin and on the open flood plain of the Alligator river, immature and adult Pied Herons were present in equal numbers.

The Australian race of the Sacred Ibis *Threskiornis aethiopicus molucca* was sitting on eggs in the colony, but both the Little Pied Cormorant *Phalacrocorax melanoleucos* and the Little Black Cormorant *P. sulcirostris* had fledged young. The Darter tended to nest along the river in trees away from the main colony, possibly because of lack of space, and all were feeding young at the nest. We had discovered the nest of the Great Billed Heron *Ardea sumatrana* a mile (1.6 km) or more up a tidal creek near Darwin; it contained one young, its scraggy neck stretched out and its bill pointing

The Intermediate Egret thrives in the colonies here.

upwards in a 'bitterning' display from the huge stick nest. Another adult was seen near the colony down the river, and it seems likely that several pairs nest solitarily in the taller trees in the dense, mangrove-lined, narrow tidal creeks. The Green (Mangrove) Heron *Butorides striatus,* which uses a similar habitat, was seen regularly, but none was in breeding plumage; the subspecies here, *stagnatilis,* is, as ever with this adaptable species, plumed to blend with its grey mudded habitat.

Around the heronry were numerous kites of several species, but predominantly Whistling *Haliastur sphenurus.* The occasional Brahminy Kite *Haliastur indus* and Brown Goshawk *Accipiter fasciatus* flew over.

There are huge numbers of birds out across the flood plain, but only at high tide, when one navigable creek leads across the grassy open marshlands, which are interspersed with drier high ground and wetter, reed-lined ponds. The most abundant is the strange Magpie Goose. Plumed Tree Ducks *Dendrocygna eytoni* were in small flocks, and pairs of Burdekin Shelducks *Tadorna radjah* had small young. Small parties of Black-necked Storks *Ephippiorhynchus asiaticus* gave aerial chase to each other, snapping with their huge bills; not all had the diagnostic red legs, but were otherwise adults in all plumage details. Flocks of egrets wheeled and turned overhead, mainly Cattle Egrets in pure white winter plumage, but small parties of non-breeding Little Egrets and a few great White Egrets were also evident.

We saw one pair of Brolgas *Grus rubicundus* and, on the dry higher

Red capped dotterel shading its eggs from the fierce heat of the sun.

The South Alligator River.

Black fronted dotterel keeps a huge eye on the camera.

Pied Heron on the nest. Surprisingly little is known about this small egret.

ground, a pair of Australian Bustards *Ardeotis australis*. Occasional Royal Spoonbills *Platalea (leucorodia) regia* were feeding along the water-channel edge. Their colony was across the plain in the paper bark trees, where there were some 200 pairs. This species has been reclassified as a race of the European Spoonbill in the new Peters' Check List, but in the absence of detailed field studies this conclusion appears premature. Certainly, the head crest on this Royal Spoonbill is more prominently displayed than in its European counterpart.

Along the sea coast, altering from rocky and sandy shore to extensive mudflats with mangrove swamps behind them, we glimpsed the occasional Black Bittern *Dupetor flavicollis*, but commoner was the Eastern Reef Heron *Egretta sacra*. Feeding solitarily along the rocky coast were both white and darkly plumed Reef Herons in about equal numbers. They gave every indication of feeding territorially, and occasionally disputes and low aerial chases ensued. Quite a different pattern of behaviour occurred within the muddy bay of Darwin Harbour. Here some 20 birds fed in close proximity to one another, appearing to have no territorial feeding areas of any appreciable size; while local disputes occurred they were not pursued and, with one Little Egret joining them, they foraged along the shoreline. As the tide flowed every effort was made to peer into the water. Two methods were used: they hung downwards from a rock or high perch, or adopted a long

Both white and dark phases of the Eastern Reef Heron are found along the coast.

crouching position with bill horizontal and parallel to the sea, and invariably with half-open wings. From these positions, crayfish and molluscs were the commonest prey taken.

During about six hours of watching on three separate days it was clear that the dark birds were not catching many fish, but the white birds were. Furthermore, the pecking order was dominated by three or four white birds. Much more detailed study than this short observation would be needed, however, before any significance could be attached to it. This group of birds was reported to nest in the wooden struts under the pier, but were not doing so when we were there. It seemed probable that some birds in this group were young of the year: both their legs and their bill were pale brown, indicating immaturity, and spring nesting in early November is likely to be the usual start of the breeding cycle here.

On the sandy shingle, both on the coast and inland, were found several species of plover, or 'dotterel' as they are named in Australia. The little Red-capped Dotterel *Charadrius ruficapillus* seemed to fill the ecological

niche of the Little Ringed Plover *C. dubius* elsewhere; this latter species is a migrant here, but does not stay to breed. We found nests with eggs, both along the shore and inland, of the Red-capped Dotterel, and one bird performed the 'broken-wing' display to deter us from approaching the nest. This interesting behaviour pattern involves the bird in a series of wing flaps while lying on the ground, feigning injury, and is designed to attract attention away from the nest. Many species perform this display, but it is most marked in plovers.

Inland, we came across the large eggs of the Masked Plover *Vanellus miles* in a small scrape, and we found the Black-fronted Plover *Charadrius melanops* common, though it evidently comes as an early winter visitor during the dry weather.

One shorebird of particular interest as a wet-season visitor is the Greytailed or Siberian Tattler *Heteroscelus brevipes*. There has been much argument as to whether it is a race of the Wandering Tattler *H. incanus* or a separate species, but it is interesting to note that the latter bird does not

Eastern Reef Herons are not related to Little Egrets as are the Western Reef Herons.

A young Pied Heron. This heron retains its white head for at least its first year. Early ornithologists thought it was a different species from its dark-headed parent.

The eggs of the Magpie Goose are favourite food for the Aborigines.

normally winter in the Top End area, but is found on the east and southeast coasts of Australia.

This wetlands area is very thinly populated: the population of Darwin is only 55 000. Eastwards, some 5684 km^2 comprise the first stage of the Kakadu National Park, now proclaimed as a World Heritage area. Much of the wildlife of the area is protected, naturally by the sheer size and inaccessibility of the region, as well as by the hazards of wild buffalo and crocodiles previously mentioned. The discovery of uranium deposits, however, and the development of mines to exploit these, has led to a new town and the danger of pollution and of the fracturing of this ecosystem which, as in all wetland areas, is delicately balanced and as yet little understood. Until the CSIRO and the Northern Territories Conservation Commission get further along with their studies of environmental problems, and the newly established Park Authorities have had time to acquire expertise in managing such a territory, there is bound to be some damage done.

Masked Plovers have large yellow wattles and are birds of the tropical north.

The Australian Little Egret has bright yellow toes and black feet.

When in Darwin, I urged, through the media, that stage 2 of the park expansion be implemented, and indeed that the whole of the South Alligator river be created a conservation area. There are no problems of inhabitants being dispossessed, there is little additional expense involved, and there are no great plans for commercial exploitation, at least not on the scale proposed in the much more heavily populated regions of Florida or Chiba Prefecture in Japan. So now is the time for far-reaching measures. Judging by the pride these Top End settlers of the Northern Territory have in their lands, it seems highly likely that such legislation will soon be enacted.

11 **Spain**

The Coto Doñana

The Parque Nacional de Doñana lies in the triangle between the Andalucian cities of Huelvos, Cadiz and Sevilla. This wetland region is formed by the delta of the River Guadalquivir, which faces southwest to the Atlantic Ocean. The gales which blow across this ocean have, over many centuries, forced back the sand from the beaches and the sediment from the delta to form a barrier which blocks the numerous tributaries, leaving only the main channel of this tidal river, which continues to deposit silt from its mouth.

Along the coast high winds move the sand closer to the tree line.

Grey Herons, Spoonbills and several species of egrets all nest in one of the great heronries in this reserve.

This material is still being pushed on to the barrier, raising the level of the marismas formed behind it. The strong tides up the river ensure the continuing salinity of the swamplands, which in turn provide the food for the numerous bird species, both resident and migratory.

Along the sandy coastal ridges, there are stone pines *Pinus pinea* which were planted some centuries ago to help to stabilize the movement of the dunes. Between the ridges are a series of freshwater-filled slacks, and immediately before the marismas the higher ground is scattered with gorse *Ulex* and broom *Halimium*, scrub and cork oaks *Quercus suber*. The richer zones have denser cover, with thickets of pistachio *Pistacea lentiscens* and bramble *Pteridium*. This luxuriant foliage is sustained by the high water table, and thus is at risk during continuous periods of drought.

This makes a diverse habitat at the closest region in Europe to North Africa, and is a major focus for the many migration routes of the African/European avifauna. It is, therefore, a haven for migratory species wintering in Africa and breeding in Europe in summer. It is also a rich winter feeding ground for the Western Palearctic ducks and wading birds. Add to this its unique resident species, such as the distinctive Spanish race of the Imperial Eagle *Aquila heliaca adalberti*, and its importance can be readily appreciated.

In western Europe only the Camargue in southern France can compare

with this region of wetlands. Like the Camargue, it owes its survival in such a heavily populated western European environment to its history. In spite of invasions and civil wars, it has been protected from the pressures of modern development and exploitation, until the last two decades, by its remoteness.

King Alfonso X made Las Rocinas, now called El Rocio, a royal hunting ground. It passed in succession to the dukes of Medina-Sidonia, who maintained it as a hunting preserve for almost 500 years. It was the wife of the seventh duke Alfonso who persuaded him to regain title of this isolated region from the Council of the town of Almonte, to whom it had passed after much legal controversy. He built a small palace for her and it became

A Squacco Heron in full breeding plumage.

Over the page: Purple Heron

known thereafter as the Palace of Doñana, named after the unhappy recluse Dona Ana.

A grey heron fishes in the marsh.

All the kings of Spain hunted wild boars and deer as guests of the dukes, using the Palacio as a hunting lodge until, at the turn of the century, ownership of the property passed to William Garvey, who leased it for hunting, after exploiting the pine timber. Abel Chapman, the famous shotgun naturalist, was one of the members of the four-man syndicate known as Sociedad de Monteros, and it is his perceptive writings in *Wild Spain* and *Unexplored Spain* which first brought wide attention to the richness of wildlife here.

By the beginning of the First World War the title had passed through marriage to the Duke of Tarifa, who, as an important Spanish sportsman, developed and managed the area for hunting, planting pine trees and additional cover for game. In 1933 the Duchess's sister, the Marquesa de Borghetto, inherited the property, retaining the southern portion and selling the remainder to three local landowners, the Marques del Merito, Don Manuel M Gonzalez and Don Salvador Noguera. Thus this key area, of vast strategical importance for resident and migratory wildlife, had remained virtually untouched and unspoilt for hundreds of years, until less than 30 years ago.

It is beyond dispute that, in the period since the early 1950s, modern

Little Grebes are common nesters. They cover the eggs in their untidy nests when they go to feed.

development, after pausing for breath following the devastation of the Second World War, quickened in pace so rapidly, and with so little pause for consideration of the long-term consequences, that the devastation wrought upon the natural environment of the world has been greater in these last three decades than in all the previous history of the world. Spain was not excluded from this. Rapid tourist development of the coastal areas of southern Spain soon led to the search for further areas to build upon. The whole of the Coto was threatened by the decision to build a road from the north to link up with a newly acquired coastal strip along the sandy beaches, in order to create a new tourist resort.

The riches of the birdlife, mammal and plant life were recorded and documented by the three expeditions to the region by Guy Mountfort, the well-known ornithologist and writer. Between 1952 and 1957 he led three parties of internationally known naturalists, who explored and analysed the fauna, flora and ecology of the region. His book *Portrait of the Wilderness*, the first of many such revelations of the world's wilderness areas, was the necessary plea for a region now under siege from all sides. It was saved in the nick of time from being totally overrun, but its future may still be uncertain.

The investigations carried out by these expeditions made it abundantly

Redshanks commonly breed here.

apparent that this remarkable wetland region was of major importance to the very survival of many of Europe's migrants. Pressure was, therefore, brought to bear from all sides to create a permanent reserve. In 1964, with considerable financial support from the World Wildlife Fund, an area was purchased for a Biological Station in the Doñana. This small beginning consisted of a region of 6794 ha, quite insufficient to sustain the needs of the creatures within such a reserve. Fortunately, in 1969 further resources made it possible to buy an additional 3214 ha, and later that year the Spanish Government decreed that 35 000 ha should be declared a National Park.

Doctor Toño Valverde was appointed the first Director of the Biological Station, then housed in the Palacio, and shortly after he was appointed I was able to visit him there. I was accompanied by Stanley Cramp, President of the BOU and Editor of the prestigious *The Birds of the Western Palearctic*, and Peter Conder, then the Director of the RSPB.

It was not until 1983 that I returned again to the Coto Doñana. I found things greatly changed. All the mistakes of modern wetland management made throughout the many world reserves are seen in retrospect as being comparatively easily avoidable. But the hindsight is of little value. Here in the Coto, mistakes of the most basic kind have been made and, added to

Griffin Vultures are the largest of the scavengers on the Coto.

these, an unprecedented series of drought years has resulted in the once-teeming wildlife population shrinking alarmingly. Exhilaration at the success of the early efforts and the apparent securing of an inviolate sanctuary has given way to concern, argument and bitter disappointment.

The difficulties of wetland conservation in highly populated regions of the world are quite apparent today. The competition for available water resources is constantly increasing. Farmers, horticulturists, city dwellers and tourists all have growing needs. Diverting water to meet these needs is invariably politically expedient. The use of pesticides and herbicides, and the resultant pollution, have grown ever greater. Finally, and paradoxically, the quite recently acquired public awareness of the danger to our wild places, and the strong conservationist movement which has resulted, have brought their own problem of how to cope with the greatly increasing numbers of visitors to such regions.

Spain is no exception to this trio of pressures, and the Coto Doñana, with its promise of high ideals, has found itself battling with all three. It is tempting to consider that isolation and neglect might have been preferable here, as it has been elsewhere, but this idealistic view cannot stand up against the tide of events in the increasingly populated world in which we live. So the problems must be faced. The great reserve of the Coto Doñana will, and must, survive, but it is no good hiding its problems: it needs support from all quarters to retain and succour its invaluable heritage.

The Spanish Imperial Eagle is a
breeding bird here amongst the larger
cork oaks, but only a very few still
survive.

Cattle Egrets in full breeding plumage form part of a large colony.

My arrival in 1983, like everything about my second visit to the Coto Doñana, was in sharp contrast to the one 18 years earlier. I came by coach to a newly erected tourist hotel at Matalascares, a town which had been built on the sand dunes since my earlier visit. From there, a Land Rover with a driver from the National Park service travelled around the park area, but was excluded from the biological reserve. I learnt that this was under entirely separate management and that separate permission was required to visit it. Eventually I was granted permission to enter, so that I could see once more the elegant Palacio, now ringed by a gravelled road, and, more importantly, to visit the famous heronry in the majestic cork oaks nearby.

This colony, when recorded by Guy Mountfort's expedition in 1956, had been further north at Bellota Garda, with some 7000 nests of four species of heron. On my first visit, in 1965, about 600 nests of three species were mostly unsuccessful, because of the drought conditions of that year. In 1983 there was great concern, as there had been little or no rainfall for a number of years, but the numbers of nests were similar: Little Egrets *Egretta garzetta* and Cattle Egrets *Bubulcus ibis* had 100 nests each; Grey Herons *Ardea cinerea* and Spoonbills *Platalea leucorodia* over 120 nests each; and Night Herons *Nycticorax nycticorax* 15 nests.

The surprise to me was the absence of Squacco Herons *Ardeola ralloides* at the nesting site. More importantly, I could find no trace of them at any of their previously well-known feeding areas. This species is usually less

affected by disturbance or water levels than other heron species. The
possibility could not be ruled out that pesticides or other crop pollution had
affected the food supply of this adaptable species.

Records show that the European Grey Heron was holding to its average
numbers over the years, but it was hard to tell why the Cattle Egret, which
was seen feeding wherever cattle were present, was breeding in such
reduced numbers. Spoonbills had not been breeding when the Mountfort
expeditions had visited the area, but some 200 nests were seen by us in
1965.

There was considerable concern among staff at the Biological Station
that there should be no disturbance while egg-laying was taking place. This
concern over disturbance is understandable, though experience of many
heron colonies indicates that careful study has little or no effect on breeding
success. The problem is invariably the Spoonbills, which as those great
conservationists the Dutch know, are the most excitable species. A careful
approach, however, can lead to complete indifference, as is the case at
Bharatpur in India.

In a reserve such as this one, visitors expect to be allowed to see
something of the spectacular sights; and it seems essential to let them do so.
Expertly erected hides, after the style of those at Minsmere in Suffolk
designed by Herbert Axell, the ex-warden of the RSPB reserve, have
succeeded beside the freshwater lagoons at Acebra and form the focal point

Flocks of Dunlins move along the
coast in spring and autumn.

Spoonbills occupy the trees in the colony.

for all groups of visitors. Quite close observation can be made, and the same techniques could also be applied at the heronry. There is, however, a sharp contrast between the priorities of the National Park authorities, who want to promote interest and tourism, and those of the Biological Station, who dislike disturbance. As a result of this conflict of interest between the two bodies, an even-handed approach is difficult to achieve.

Conservation must naturally work within the political environment as well as the natural environment. At El Rocio, the natural marshland bordering the town is a well-fenced area of the National Park. Many wetland birds feed there, though many fewer were seen in 1983 than previously, and no nesting was observed. A few Greater Flamingoes *Phoenicopterus ruber* visited the swamp in the evenings. Black-winged Stilts *Himantopus himantopus* were present, as were transient Black-tailed Godwits *Limosa limosa*. Whiskered Terns *Chlidonias hybridus* dived for fish in the narrow water channels. In contrast, the reeds across the main road, outside the reserve, contained Purple Herons *Ardea purpurea*, Little Bitterns *Ixobrychus minutus* and Great Reed Warblers *Acrocephalus arundinaceus*, all of which were undoubtedly breeding, as were the Red-rumped Swallows *Hirundo daurica* under the bridge.

The problem in this area of the reserve is caused by numbers of cattle,

The Palacio de Doñana is now a visitor centre.

sheep and horses which eat the vegetation, and by riders who move freely about to herd them. Around the channels were nets to catch crayfish, and local fishermen used a gap in the fence to fish within the reserve. It would seem to be politically inexpedient to exclude traditional local interests, but El Rocio benefits greatly from tourists, who come not only for the annual religious festival and the beautiful church but also to see the wildlife, so that such considerations must be given thought and the problem must eventually be tackled.

There was an international camera crew nearby. I had met some of them elsewhere in the world making wildlife films for television. They had obviously received permission to go anywhere and to do what they wished, apparently without supervision. Roll after tangled roll of discarded film in huge quantities was scattered indiscriminately around the reserve. Such behaviour is becoming more and more common as the box-office appeal of films about wildlife increases. The damage that can be done by such irresponsible groups is far-reaching, and must at some stage outweigh the advantage of creating among the general public an awareness of wildlife and of the need to conserve it. Litter is but one of the indicators of a general lack of scruples, and the need for close supervision is very apparent. Apart from the immediate damage, it provides a very poor impression for others.

The dryness of this season, as indeed of that of my previous visit, meant that most passage migrants were absent from the reserve, though there were large flocks of Black-tailed Godwits on several pools. The main movement of shorebirds was along the lower stretches of the Guadalquivir river, and here we saw Dunlins *Calidris alpina*, Grey Plovers *Pluvialis squatarola* resplendent in full 'black-bellied' plumes, Curlew Sandpipers *Calidris ferruginea*, Ruffs *Philomachus pugnax*, Redshanks *Tringa totanus*, Spotted Redshanks *T. erythropus*, Turnstones *Arenaria interpres* and Little Stints *Calidris minuta*. Large restless parties of Ringed Plovers *Charadrius hiaticula* were flying in purposeful, tightly packed formation, obviously intent on the next stage to their more northerly breeding grounds. On the

A Cattle Egret raises its honey-buff crest in annoyance.

Hoopoe.

sandy shore were Oystercatchers *Haematopus ostralegus*, Sanderlings *Calidris alba* and flocks of immature gulls Larus spp.

On the lagoons, Moorhens *Gallinula chloropus* were sitting on eggs and Coots *Fulica atra* already feeding young. On the marsh edge, the harsh voice of the Great Reed Warbler competed with the melodious but insistent song of the Nightingale *Luscinia megarhynchos*. Hoopoes *Upupa epops* and Rollers *Coracias garrulus* called from the shrubland and Bee-eaters *Merops apiaster* sat on the telephone wires, newly erected since my previous visit.

There were wonderful sights to be seen and for those unfamiliar with the area it was indeed a rare experience. Everywhere, however, there were signs of increasing urban development, and the former trackless wilderness was criss-crossed with paths and roads; motor cars, containing importantly suited men, hurried past with genial waves. It was a sharp contrast to the dignified trot of the lone mounted Guardia of earlier days. A few Pratincoles *Glareola pratincola* swooped over, but the huge flocks were missing. A Dartford Warbler *Sylvia undata* was found, and a single Great Grey Shrike *Lanus excubitor* of the pink-breasted southern race *meridionalis*. Nowhere were there the numbers of birds described by Guy Mountford in *Portrait of a Wilderness*. He reports Max Nicholson's count in 100 acres (40 ha) as being 1891 birds of 35 species seen in one day. This number of species is still present, but there is certainly no opportunity to record them in such numbers now.

Let us hope that the efforts of the dedicated Spanish scientists and Park wardens will succeed in striking and maintaining a balance between the different demands placed upon them, so that this most precious of European wetlands can remain an ornithological refuge.

The Marismas de Hinogos is now a virtual dust-bowl, and along the artificial lagoons discarded shotgun cartridges lie wherever there are ducks and wading birds congregated. There is news that some of the diverted water supplies used for the rapidly expanding cultivation of these lands may be allowed to flow back across the Marismas. Until now the diverted water has, after use, flowed back into the main river channel and thus been lost to the sea. Some of this can now hopefully also be recycled into the Park.

The Florida Everglades had almost exactly similar experiences, and for many years had problems which much resemble those of the Coto Doñana. There can never be the vast expenditure employed here as was ultimately needed to correct early mistakes in south Florida, but a few imaginative schemes carried out now could save the situation from further rapid deterioration which, if allowed to continue, may not be capable of reversal.

12 Iceland

Lake Mývatn – The Land of the Midges

In the north-east of Iceland, Lake Mývatn plays host to probably the largest concentration of breeding ducks in the world. No fewer than 15 species breed here. Three species of American waterbirds have their European nesting outposts here. Harlequin Ducks *Histrionicus histrionicus* (found nowhere else in Europe), Barrow's Golden Eye *Bucaphala islandica* with 800 pairs on the lake, and the Great Northern Diver *Gavia immer*, better known by its American name of Common Loon, are joined in early spring, as the seven-month-long winter ice melts, by tens of thousands of European duck, waders, grebes, and that harbinger of spring, the Golden Plover *Pluvialis apricaria*. By the lake side and on the surrounding hills Greylag *Anser anser* and Pinkfooted geese *Anser brachyrhynchus* nest, as does the Whooper Swan *Cygnus cygnus*.

The lake feeds the fast-flowing River Laxá as it heads northward to the Atlantic Ocean. A huge area around Lake Mývatn was given nature reserve status when no less than 440,000 hectares was officially designated in 1974. This effectively banned shooting or trapping, but the age-old practice of egg collecting still continues. Tradition demands that in each nest a minimum of four eggs must be left, and this has been maintained by local farm-

Lava formations on Lake Mývatn.

Harlequin Duck and Drake.

Oystercatcher is a common
breeder in Iceland.

Above. Slavonian Grebe.
Below. A Redwing enjoys a bath.

Whooper Swans, most are non-breeders.

Long-tailed Ducks, the male has a pink bill with a black tip.

Top. Red-necked Phalarope seem to
nest on every point around the lake.
Bottom. A male Eider. Eider are
found higher up the Laxá river.

Arctic Tern breed here in large
numbers.

Next page. Barrow's Goldeneye.
The females have red bills and brown
heads.

Black-tailed Godwit in full
breeding plumage.

Tufted Duck with young, a common species here.

Icelandic farmer's wife at a nest. She will guard hundreds of nests here after collecting her share of eggs.

Sulphur Lake.

ers and has meant that the heavy concentration of all species remains intact. Slavonian Grebe *Podiceps auritus*, Arctic Tern *Sterna paradisaea*, Red-necked Phalarope *Phalaropus lobatus*, Redwing *Turdus iliacus*, Whimbrel *Numenius phaeopus* and even Red Throated Divers *Gavia stellata* are more numerous here than anywhere else in Europe.

Between the middle of May to the middle of July the north-west shore and all the numerous islands on the lake are out of bounds. there are about six hundred Icelanders in the whole area, and whilst many visitors come during the breeding, they are not allowed to stray on to farmer's land which is jealously guarded.

During the summer millions of midges emerge from the lake to form large swarms. The less numerous but painful biting black fly also make their presence known. All these insects are the main diet of the hatchlings and help to account for the quite un-precedented numbers and diversity of duck to be found here.

Besides the birds, fish such as char, trout, and most importantly, the largest salmon in Iceland that run up the Laxá river feed on this super abundant insect life.

All around the lake are pools of sulphur, and the barren land is littered with pseudo-craters and a multitude of volcanic craters. Such is the landscape that the first American astronauts trained here in preparation for moon landings. Spectacular lava architecture make the scenery of the lake a photographers dream. Add to this the fifty islands of lake and over 100 000 .birds present at any one time, and you have a sight worth seeing.

Further reading

I have here given suggestions for further reading and advice on what guide books to consult for each region. For all the areas there is much more detailed information, and this can be obtained by studying the scientific literature, popular magazines (which often have excellent articles by visiting ornithologists) and by careful research in the specialist libraries. As with travel advice, further assistance can often be had by writing to the authors of books on birds of the area to be visited.

The Florida Everglades

Peterson, Roger Tory. 1946. *A Field Guide to the Birds, including all Species found in Eastern America*. Houghton Mifflin, New York.
This splendid guide is all you really need, but a checklist of the birds of the Everglades National Park compiled by John Ogden can be purchased at the Park headquarters.

If you are a very serious student, obtain Report T-514, *A Bibliography of South Florida Wading Birds*, published by the South Florida Research Center, PO Box 279, Homestead, Florida 33030.

Northern Argentina

de Schauensee, R. Mayer. 1971. *A Guide to the Birds of South America*. Oliver Boyd, London. In English.
Olrog, Claus Chr. 1959. *Las Aves Argentinas*. Universidad Nacional de Tucumán. Instituto 'Miguel Lillo'. In Spanish but with very poor illustrations.
Nores, Manuel & Yzurieta, Dario. 1980. *Aves de Ambientes Acuaticos de Cordoba y Centro de Argentina*. Secretaria de Estado de Agricultura y Ganoderia. Direccion de Caza, Pesea y Actividades Acuaticas. This is the latest Spanish book on waterbirds, with good illustrations.

For the serious student:
Short, Lester L. 1975. *A Zoological Analysis of the South American Chaco Avifauna*. Bulletins of the American Museum of Natural History, vol. 154, article 3. New York.
N. Gardner and D Gardner. 1990. *A Birder's Guide to Travel in Argentine*

The Tana River, Kenya

Williams, John G. & Arlott, Norman. 1980. *A Field Guide to the Birds of East Africa*. Collins, London.

Zimmerman D. D., Turner D., Pearson I,. & Pratt D. 1996 *Birds of Kenya and Northern Tanzania*. Christopher Helm
For in-depth study, the following books are highly recommended.
Mackworth-Praed, C. W. & Grant, C. H. B. 1957. *African Handbook of Birds. Series I Vols 1 & 2. Birds of Eastern & North Eastern Africa*. Longmans, London & New York.
Brown, L. H., Urban, E. K., & Newman, K. 1982. *The Birds of Africa. Vols 1–5*. Academic Press, London & New York. With volumes 6 and 7 to come.

If you are serious about the game animals read:
Kingdon, J. 1971–82. *East African Mammals. An Atlas of Evolution in Africa*. Academic Press, London & New York. Seven books in three volumes.

Kingdon, J. 1997. *Kingdon Field Guide to African Mammals*. Academic Press, San Diego and London.

For travel buy the AA book when in Nairobi and contact the East African Wildlife Society, Mezzanine Floor, Nairobi Hilton Building, tel: 27047/331888. Six times a year they issue SWARA, which is a splendid magazine full of information and useful advertisements.

Bharatpur

There is no fully comprehensive field guide. The best series is, of course:
Ali, S. & Dillon Ripley, S. 1968. *Handbook of the Birds of India and Pakistan*. Oxford University Press. 10 volumes.
Ewans, M. 1989. *Bharatpur, Bird Paradise*. HF & G Witherby Ltd, London.
Sankhala, K. 1990. *Garden of God*. Vikas Publishing House Pvt. Ltd, New Delhi.

Field guides are:
Ali, Sálim. 1979. *The Book of Indian Birds*. Eleventh Edition. Bombay Natural History Society.
Woodcock, Martin. 1980. *Collins Handguide to the Birds of the Indian Sub-continent*. Collins. London.

Growal Bikram 1997. *Birds of the Indian Sub-Continent*. Odyssey

There are also checklists available at the Forest Lodge.

Gujarat

Dharmakumarsingh R. S. *Birds of Sarrashtra*. This privately published book is very rare today.

Assam

Hancock, J., Kushlan, J. & Kahl, M. P. 1994. *Storks, Ibises & Spoonbills of the World*. Academic Press, London.

The Zhalong Reserve, Heilanchiang Province

Arthur Probesthain, 4 Great Russell Street, London WC1, stocks a very wide range of books about China. Bird guides, however, need to be obtained from a specialist natural history bookshop. The following are the important ones:
Cheng Tso-hsin. 1976. *Distributional List of Chinese Birds*. Peking Institute of Zoology, Academia Sinica. (In Chinese with scientific names in Latin and

distributional maps.)

Etchécoper, R. D. & Hüe, F. 1978 & 1982. *Les Oiseaux de Chine*. 2 vols. (In French with many colour plates.)

Gore, M. E. J. & Pyong-oh Won. 1971. *The Birds of Korea*. Charles E. Tuttle & Co., Tokyo. (In English and Korean. Now out of print.)

King B., Woodcock, M. & Dickinson, E. C. 1975. *A Field Guide to the Birds of South East Asia*. Collins, London. (More than 70 per cent of the species likely to be seen are illustrated.)

Wilder, G. D. & Hubbard, H. W. 1938. *Birds of Northeastern China*. Peking Natural History Bulletin Handbook 6: 614–628 and others.

Wild Bird Society of Japan. 1982. *A Field Guide to the Birds of Japan*. UK Agents are SOC Bookshop, Edinburgh. (In English. Essential: the text and illustrations are of a very high standard and cover the majority of species found in the area.

The Shinhama Reserve, Chiba, Tokyo

ESSENTIAL READING

Wild Bird Society of Japan. 1982. *A Field Guide to the Birds of Japan*. Tokyo. This guide is available in Europe from the SOC Bookshop, 21 Regent Terrace, Edinburgh EH7 5BT, Scotland, telephone 0131 556 6042. In addition to a most comprehensive guide and bibliography, it contains an excellent chapter on where to watch birds in Japan. A more detailed guide to birdwatching localities is also available (in Japanese) by applying to the headquarters of the Wild Bird Society of Japan at Aoyama Flower Building, 1-1-4 Shibuya, Shibuya-ku, Tokyo 150.

Brazil M. 1991. *The Birds of Japan*. Christopher Helm

Pulau Dua, Indonesia

Hancock, J. A. Kushlan, J. A. & Kahl, M. P. 1992. *Storks, Ibises and Spoonbills of the World*. Academic Press, London.

King, B., Woodcock, M. & Dickinson, E. C. 1975. *A Field Guide to the Birds of South East Asia*. Collins, London.

MacKinnon, J. & Phillipps, K. 1993. *A Field Guide to the Birds of Borneo, Sumatra, Java & Bali*. Oxford Univeristy Press, Oxford.

There are two useful handbooks from nearby areas:

Tweedie, M. W. F. 1960. *Common Malayan Birds*. In the Malayan Nature Handbooks series. Longmans, London.

Beehler, Bruce McP. 1978. *Upland Birds of Northeastern New Guinea*. Wau Ecology Institute. Handbook No. 4.

And finally a book in Dutch with excellent illustrations:

Hoogerwerf, A. 1949. *De Avifauna van de Plantentuin te Buitenzory (Java)*. De Kon. Plantentuin van Indonesie, Buitenzory, Java.
This last consists of a full list of birds in the botanical gardens.

Darwin and the South Alligator River

There is more literature available here than anywhere else with the possible exception of Florida. Two first-class field guides are:

Pizzey, Graham. 1998. *A Field Guide to the Birds of Australia* (2nd edition). Collins, London.

Slater, Peter. 1971. *A Field Guide to Australian Birds*. 2 vols. Oliver & Boyd, London.

Marchant et al. 1994. *The Handbook of Australian, New Zealand and Antarctic Birds*. R. A. C. U.

The Coto Doñana, Spain

These are countless books aimed at birdwatchers in Europe. One of the best is:
Peterson, R. T., Mountfort, G. & Hollom, P. 1983. *A Field Guide to the Birds of Britain and Europe* (5th edition). Collins, London.

For a detailed account of Coto Doñana, the following is essential:
Mountfort, Guy. 1958. *Portrait of a Wilderness*. Hutchinson, London.

Lake Myvatn, Iceland

Bardarson, H. R. 1986. *Birds of Iceland*. Reykjavik§
T. Einarsson 1991. *Guide to the Birds of Iceland*. A practical Handbook for Identification.

East Africa

Zimmerman, Dale, Turner, Don, Pearson, David, Willis, Ian, and Pratt, Douglas. 1996. *Birds of Kenya and Northern Tanzania*.

Argentina

Narosky, T. and Yzurieta, D. 1989. 2nd edition. *Birds of Argentina and Uraguay*.

USA

The Audubon Society Master Guide to Birding. 1984. Vols 1–3. Series Editor John Farrand Jr. Knopf, USA.
Birds of North America. Collins Pocket Guide. 1993.
A Field Guide to the Birds of North America. National Geographic Society. 1987.

There are, of course, dozens more!!

Finally as the new literature piles up go to Web catalogue http://www.nhbs.com

Index

Blanco, Dr Claudio 32
Borghetto, Marquesa de 143
Boselaphus tragocamelus 64
Boswall, Jeffery 102
Botaurus lentiginosus see
Bittern, American
Botaurus stellaris see Bittern,
Eurasian
box-jellyfish 128
Brolga 131
Brookfield, Charles M. 1
broom 140
Bubalus bubalis 128
Bubulcus ibis 21, 37, 38, 71,
148, **148**, 149, **152**
Bubulcus ibis coromandus see
57, 109, 110, **114**, 120–1,
128, 131
Bucephala islandica see
Goldeneye, Barrow
Bucerus leadbetteri see
Hornbill, Ground
Buffalo, water 50, 128, **129**
Bull, Blue 64
Bunting
  European Reed 101
  Japanese 101
Busarellus nigricollis see
Hawk, Black-collared
Bustard
  Australian 133
  Great 101
Buteogallus urubitinga see
Hawk, Great Black
Butorides striatus atricapillus
41
Butorides striatus stagnatilis
131
Butorides striatus virescens 13

Cairina moschata see Duck,
Muscovy
Calidris alba see Sanderling
Calidris alpina see Dunlin
Calidris ferruginea see
Sandpiper, Curlew
Calidris minuta see Stint,
Little
Calidris subminuta see Stint,
Long-toed
Callitris 125
*Calyptorhynchus magnificus
see* Cockatoo, Red-tailed
Black
Capybara 28
Caracara
  Chimango 21
  Crested 21, 27
Caracyps atratus see Vulture,
Black
Cathartes aura see Vulture,
Turkey
Cervus unicolor 64

Ceryle rudis see Kingfisher,
Pied
Chapman, Abel 143
Charadrius hiaticula see
Plover, Ringed
Charadrius melanops see
Plover, Black-fronted
Charadrius mongolus see
Plover, Lesser
(Mongolian) Sand
Charadrius ruficapillus see
Dotterel, Red-capped
Chat, Yellow 128
Chauna torquata see
Screamer, Southern
Cheke, Dudley 104
Cheke, Mrs Dudley 105,
107
Cheng Hso-tsin, Dr 98, 102
Cheng, Dr 102
Chimango 21
Chiropsalmus 128
Chlidonias hybridus see Tern,
Whiskered
Chlidonias leucopterus see
Tern, White-winged Black
Chlidonias niger see Tern,
Black
Ciconia ciconia see Stork,
European White
Ciconia (ciconia) boyciana see
Stork, Oriental White
Ciconia episcopus see Stork,
White-necked
(Woollynecked)
Circus aeruginosus see
Harrier, Marsh
Circus cyaneus see Harrier,
Hen
Circus macrourus see Harrier,
Pallid
Circus melanoleucus see
Harrier, Pied
Clangula hyamalis see Duck,
Long-tailed
Cochlearius cochlearius see
Heron, Boat-billed
Cockatoo, Red-tailed Black
128
Combretum constructum 35
Conder, Peter 145
Convolvulus 114
Coot 52, 61, 101
Coracias benghalensis see
Roller, Indian
Coracias garrulus see Roller
Cormorant
  Common (Great) 39,
56
    Double-crested **12**, 16
    Javanese Pygmy 122
    Little Black 122, 130
    Little Pied 130

Long-tailed 39
Pygmy 122
Cotton Tree 88
Cramp, Stanley 145
Crane
  Common 54, 97
  Crowned **38**
  Demoiselle 54, 96
  Eastern Sarus 122
  Hooded 98, 99
  Red-crowned **91–4**, 92,
96, **98**
  Sarus 64
  Siberian White 52, 54,
57–8, 64, 98, 99
  White-naped 96, 97, **98**
  Whooping 52–3
Crocodile, Saltwater 127,
129
Crocodylus porosus 127
Crotophaga ani see Ani,
Smooth-billed
Curlew, Far Eastern 127
Curzon, Lord 49
Cygnus cygnus see Swan
Whooper
Cypress, Bald **1**

Darter
  African 39
  Indian 60
  Oriental 122, 128, 130
de Leon, Ponce 2
Dendrocygna autumnalis see
Duck, Black-bellied Tree
Dendrocygna eytoni see Duck,
Plumed Tree
Dendrocygna javanica see
Duck, Whistling
Dendrocygna viduata see
Duck, White-faced
Devil Tree 88
Diver
  Great Northern 155
  Red Throated 165
Dotterel
  Black-fronted *see*
Plover, Black-fronted
  Red-capped **131**, 134,
135
Duck
  Black-bellied Tree 27
  Harlequin 155, **157**
  Long-tailed **159**
  Mandarin **105**, 111
  Mottled 17
  Muscovy 27
  Plumed Tree 131
  Spotbill 111
  Tufted 111, **164**
  Whistling **63**
  White-faced Tree 27
Dunlin **149**, 151

Hawk
    Black-collared 27
    Crane 27
    Great Black 27
    Savanna 27
Heron
    Black 37, **40**
    Black-crowned night
    21, 37, 38, 57, 109, 117,
    117, 121, 148
    Black-headed **42**
    Boat-billed 117
    Cocoi 21, **23**, 28
    Eastern Reef 14, **67–9**,
    71–6, **71–6**, 120, 133,
    134–5
    Great-billed 130
    Great Blue 8, 15, **23**
    Green (Green-backed;
    Mangrove) 13, 41, 131
    Grey 37, 56, 95, 121–2,
    140, **143**, 148, **149**
    Indian Pond 57, 57
    Javanese Pond **120**, 121
    Little Blue 14, **15**, 130
    Nankeen Night 121,
    128
    Pied 128, 130, **133**, **136**
    Purple 37, **37**, 38, 56,
    95, 121, 122, **142**, 150
    Rufescent Tiger **21–2**,
    30
    Squacco 37, **141**, 148
    Tricolor (Louisiana)
    10, 14
    Western Reef 41, 43,
    59–60
    Whistling 21, **25**, 28, **28**
    Yellow-crowned Night
    6–7
Heteroscelus brevipes see
    Tattler, Grey-tailed
Heteroscelus incanus see
    Tattler, Wandering
Heterospizias meridionalis see
    Hawk, Savanna
Himantopus himantopus see
    Stilt, Black-winged
Himantopus mexicanus see
    Stilt, Black-necked
Hirundo daurica see Swallow,
    Red-rumped
Hirundo rustica see Swallow,
    European
Histrionicus histrionicus see
    Duck, Harlequin
Hoopoe **153**
Hornbill, Ground **36–7**
Hudson, W.H. 19, 22
Hydrochoerus hydrochaeris 28
Hydrophasianus chirurgus see
    Jacana, Pheasant-tailed

Ianas acuta see Pintail
Ibis
    Asiatic 71
    Australian Sacred **126**,
    130
    Black 57, 71, **80**
    Buff-necked **22**, 27
    Glossy 17, 26, 39, 57,
    122
    Hadada **36–7**
    Oriental White **54–5**,
    57, **62**, 95, 122
    Plumbeous 27
    Sacred 39, 57, 130
    Straw-necked 128
    White 5, 10, 17
    White-faced Glossy 21
Ixobrychus eurhythmus see
    Bittern, Schrenck's
Ixobrychus exilis see Bittern,
    Least
Ixobrychus minutus see
    Bittern, European Little
Ixobrychus sinensis see
    Bittern, Chinese Yellow
    (Long-nosed)

Jacana, African 43
    Bronze-winged 61, **63**
    Pheasant-tailed 61
Jay, Plush-capped **30**
Jubiru mycteria see Stork,
    Jabiru

Keda 88
Kestrel 64
Khal, Dr Philip 86
Kingfisher, Pied **45–6**, 64
Kite
    Black (Pariah) 61
    Brahminy 122, **123**,
    131
    Everglade (Small) 10,
    13, 24
    Whistling 131
Kushlan, Dr James 10

*Lanus excubitor meridionalis
    see* Shrike, Great Grey
Lapwing 101
    Long-toed **39**
    Red-wattled 50
    Southern 21, **21**
Larus 153
Larus argentatus see Gull,
    Herring
Larus atricilla see Gull,
    Laughing
Larus maculipennis see Gull,
    Brown-headed
Leptoptilos crumeniferus see
    Stork, Marabou
Leptoptilos dubius see Stork,

Adjutant and Greater
    Adjutant
Leptoptilos javanicus see
    Stork, Lesser Adjutant
Limosa limosa see Godwit,
    Black-tailed
Limpkin 11, 28, **28–9**
Linlithgow, Lord 49
Lizard, Monitor 61, 122
Loon, Common *see* Diver,
    Great Northern
Luscinia calliope see
    Rubythroat, Siberian
Luscinia megarhynchos see
    Nightingale

Ma Yiching, Professor 96
MacDonald, Dr 102
Mallard 64
Marsh Grass 50
McClure, Dr Elliott 52
Melaleuca leucadendron 125
Merito, Marques del 143
Merops apiaster see Bee-eater
Metopidius indicus see Jacana,
    Bronze-winged
Milvago chimango see
    Caracara, Chimango
Milvus migrans see Kite,
    Black (Pariah)
Moorhen 101, 153
Mountfort, Guy 144, 148,
    154
Mycteria americana see
    Stork, Wood
Mycteria cinerea see Stork,
    Milky
Mycteria ibis see Stork,
    Yellow-billed
Mycteria leucocephalus see
    Stork, Painted
Myiopsitta monachus see
    Parakeet, Monk

Naik, Professor R.M. 73, 75
Netta peposaca see Pochard,
    Rosy-billed
Netta rufina see Pochard,
    Red-crested
Nettapus coromandelianus see
    Teal, Cotton
Nicholson, Max 154
Nycticorax violaceus see
    Heron, Yellow-crowned
    Night
Nightingale 153
Noguera, Don Salvador 143
*Numenius madagascariensis
    see* Curlew, Far Eastern
Numenius phaeopus see
    Whimbrel
Nycticorax caledonicus see
    Heron, Nankeen Night

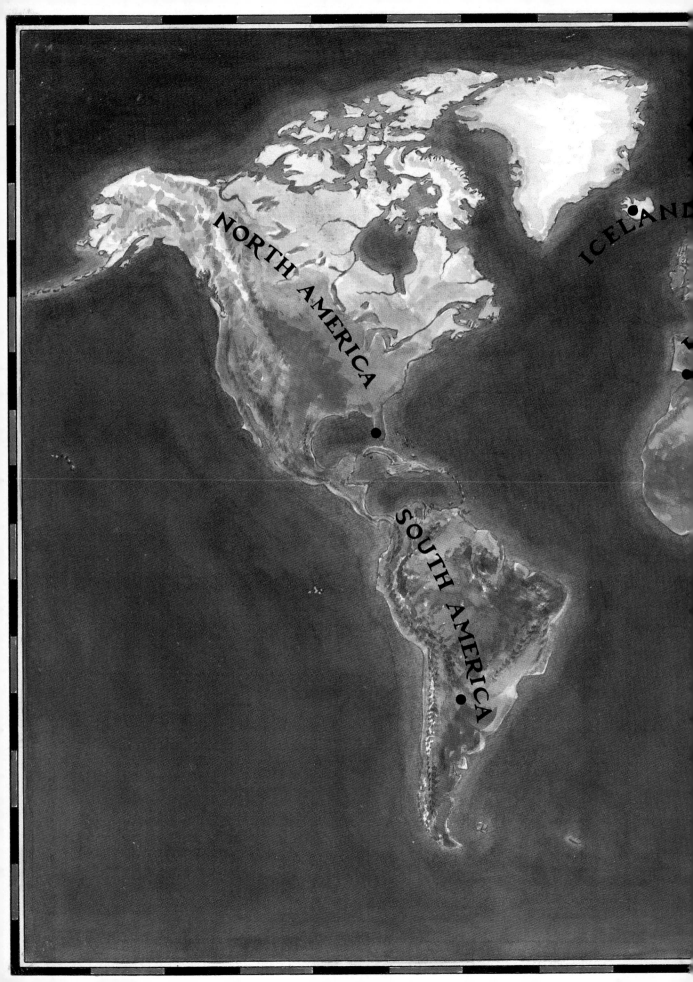